Hey, That's Our Church!

Hey, That's Our Church!

LYLE E. SCHALLER

Nashville - ABINGDON PRESS - New York

HEY, THAT'S OUR CHURCH!

Library of Congress Cataloging in Publication Data

SCHALLER, LYLE E.
 Hey, That's our church!
 1. Church management. I. Title.
 BV652.S293   254   74-17094

ISBN 0-687-16955-0

Portions of this book are based on material which first appeared in six periodicals. Grateful acknowledgment is made to the following publications:

Church Administration, for "What's Ahead for the Ex-Rural Church?" (January 1974). Copyright © 1973 The Sunday School Board of the Southern Baptist Convention. All rights reserved. Reprinted by permission.

The Interpreter, for "Getting Off the Plateau" (July-August 1973). Copyright 1973 by the Joint Committee on Communications of The United Methodist Church. Reprinted by permission.

Your Church, for "How Contemporary Is Your Church?" (May-June 1974). Copyright 1974 by the Religious Publishing Company. Reprinted by permission.

United Methodists Today, for "What's Ahead for the Saturday Evening Post Church?" (January 1974). Copyright © 1973 by The United Methodist Publishing House. Reprinted by permission.

Church School, for "Is There a Future for the Adult Sunday School Class?" (February 1975). Copyright © 1974 by Graded Press. Reprinted by permission.

Search, for "What Is Community?" (Winter 1974). Copyright © 1973 The Sunday School Board of the Southern Baptist Convention. All rights reserved. Reprinted by permission.

The Lutheran, for "Your Church Needs a Hungry Wolf" (October 2, 1974). Copyright 1974 by *The Lutheran,* magazine of the Lutheran Church in America. Reprinted by permission.

Manufactured by the Parthenon Press at
Nashville, Tennessee, United States of America

To
Josephine and Philip Deever

Contents

Introduction

At the close of the interview the forty-three-year-old minister leaned back in his chair in the study of the church and asked, "If you've a few more minutes, I would like to raise a personal question with you. What kind of jobs are open outside the church for a man like me? You know me and you know my background. Do you have any suggestions on what I might do to make a living if I were to leave the pastorate?"

While the visitor silently reflected on the question, the pastor continued, "This is my fourth pastorate. I've been here slightly less than two years now, and it's obvious that I'm a failure. The membership was declining when I came and it's continuing to decline. Worship attendance has been dropping for over a decade, and it's dropped another 15 percent in these two years. The year before I came they were short $4,000 in meeting the budget, and the first year I was here we missed it by $5,000. This year we pared the budget to the bone and we'll still be short over $2,000. The Sunday school is falling to pieces and we've received four new members in twenty-two months. Deaths and transfers out have totalled nearly fifty in that same period.

"While we've known each other for only a few years," continued the pastor, "I happen to know you have a firsthand acquaintance with each of the three churches I served before coming here. While I have not been the most successful pastor in the world, I think I did a good job for each of those three congregations. I worked hard, I learned a lot, and I don't believe I ever will have to apologize to anyone for my ministry in those three churches."

At this point he rose from his chair and began to pace nervously around the spacious study with its booklined walls. Finally he stopped, and while looking out the window, continued, "Since I came here I have tried every idea, technique, procedure, methodology, approach, gimmick, and skill I've ever learned. None of them works! We simply cannot reach the people who live in this neighborhood. Methods I've used before to make contact with newcomers that always worked for me have failed completely. Every idea I've proposed has failed. Every effort we've undertaken to reach people outside the church has been an absolute bust!"

As he continued to speak his voice became more emotional and with obvious reluctance he continued, "My wife and I have talked about this and prayed about this for months, and while she has been very supportive and encouraging, I might as well face it. I'm washed up. I've had it. I think the best thing for me to do is to leave this church so they can get someone who can help turn things around. And, frankly, when I leave here, I guess the best thing for me to do is to leave the ministry. When we came here I looked forward to another twenty-five years in the pastorate. Now, however, I believe the most responsible course of action for me to follow would be to leave the ministry. There's no point in imposing a proven failure on another congregation. What do you think?"

What do you think?

What is the most helpful perspective to use in looking at this pastor's dilemma? What approach might be helpful to him? What is an appropriate frame of reference to use in trying to understand this situation?

The most widely used approach and the one illustrated by the preceding paragraphs can be described by a very brief phrase, "Personalize and scapegoat." Whenever events do not follow in the hoped for sequence, the easiest explanation is to identify a person or group who is to blame and make that person or group the scapegoat. This procedure has been widely used in international relations, in community organization, in the Watergate fiasco, in the energy crisis, in defining the reason for the increase in the number of persons receiving public assistance, in describing the tensions which emerge when for the first time a young congregation adds a second minister to the staff, or in defining why "that" congregation is growing so rapidly and "ours" is declining in size.

This approach is deeply rooted in events and doctrines described in both the Old Testament and the New Testament. This approach rarely is creative or productive. A more helpful approach is to analyze the situation and try to discover the factors and variables that have combined to produce the dilemma.

The central thesis of this book is that analysis is not only more productive than scapegoating, but that one means of reducing the tendency to scapegoat is to encourage analysis. In more specific terms, this volume is an attempt to suggest that looking at congregations by types or categories can both inhibit the temptation to scapegoat and also produce some useful insights. This point can be illustrated by returning to the career decision facing this pastor. Is he really "washed up"? Has he actually been a complete failure? Should he leave the professional ministry?

It may be more helpful in responding to these questions to shift from a perspective of self-abasement to looking at his career in terms of the types of churches he had served. His first pastorate was as the minister and the only paid staff member of a congregation in a small town. It was the only mainline Protestant church in the community of 400 residents. After three years he moved approximately one hundred miles to a larger congregation in a city of 2900 residents. It was one of six mainline Protestant congregations in that city, but the only one of that denomination. After six satisfying years he moved eighty miles to a larger congregation in a county seat city with a population of 8,000. The congregation he served there for seven very happy years was one of eight mainline Protestant congregations serving not only that city, but also a very prosperous farming community beyond the city limits. It was by far the larger of the two congregations of his denomination in the city and also the largest of the eight in the county.

Thus for sixteen fruitful, productive, and enjoyable years this minister served as the pastor of three congregations which, while substantially different in size, were similar in many other respects. One of the important similarities was that in each place the cultural values and community context were supportive of the values and organizational life of the churches he served. Many of the church members in each of these congregations had been born and reared in that community. They grew up in a community in which the several voluntary associations identified, recruited, trained, and placed leaders who moved from a leadership position in one voluntary association to a leadership position in one of the other voluntary associations. The church was one of these voluntary associations which trained, and utilized, and exchanged with other organizations this "homegrown" volunteer leadership. While there were conflicts over schedules, the public schools and the churches regarded each other as allies and shared many of the same values and also provided leadership for each other. Many church members saw one another on frequent occasions during the week as well as on Sunday. Many worked together every day. While the membership of the churches reflected social class lines more clearly than geographical boundaries, in each of these three communities the boundaries of the parish, in terms of the place of residence of the members, coincided with the community boundaries. In the first two communities the parsonage was located next to the church building. In the third it was three blocks away. In all three, however, the

12

pastor's neighbors included members of the congregation and in all three the congregation's neighbors also were the pastor's neighbors.

At forty-one years of age and in his seventeenth year in the ministry this pastor moved to Trinity Church located in a city with a population of 165,000. Trinity was one of eight congregations of that denomination in this metropolitan area. Once it had been the prestige church of that denomination in the city. The meeting place was located about a mile west of the central business district in what had been, up until World War II, the best residential neighborhood in the city. The congregation had peaked in size once in the 1920s and again very briefly in the early 1950s, when it was served by an exceptionally able minister who was a great preacher and had a magnetic personality. He was the best known and most popular clergyman in the city. When he left in 1954, the decline began. Two decades later Trinity was an upper middle-class drive-in congregation with a meeting place in what had become a lower middle-class neighborhood. Out of a worship attendance of 180 on a typical Sunday morning, less than twenty lived within a mile of the building. More than one-half lived at least five miles away. At least 130 of that 180 had already celebrated their fiftieth birthdays and for some that event was a part of the distant past. During the twenty-two months this pastor had been here the church had been broken into by vandals at least nineteen different times. The ancient parsonage, which had been located next to the church building, had been razed several years earlier in order to enlarge the parking lot. The new eleven-year-old parsonage was located on the north side of town in a "good neighborhood" about four miles away.

Without going into further detail about Trinity it should now be clear to the reader what had happened to this pastor. He had trained, apprenticed, and gained over sixteen years of experience in what were three congregations of similar types. He then moved to a radically different type of situation. This analysis suggests that instead of identifying himself as the scapegoat in this situation and asking, "Should I leave the pastorate?" it might have been more productive to have asked, "Where does a minister with twenty years of potentially effective years of service ahead of him go for retraining when he finds himself in a completely different type of church than he has ever served before?"

Imagine for a moment, if you will please, that this minister had been born and reared in a German-speaking community, had gone only to German language schools, had served three German language parishes in German-speaking communities, and then had moved to a Portuguese-language community to serve an Italian-speaking congregation. Do you believe that some people might suggest that he should have additional training in languages if he expected to have anything but a frustrating experience in this fourth pastorate? It may be helpful to turn to two other analogies in this attempt to describe the basic assumption and the central purpose of this book.

In 1940 William Sheldon pioneered the concept of classifying people by body type. This procedure, called somatotyping, identifies three basic body types which can be defined as the spherical person, the thin person, and the Hercules type. Every person, according to Sheldon, has a bit of all three types. In a typical gathering of field and track athletes, for example, the shotputters will have a body type which is predominantly the Hercules (mesomorph) type. The runners are predominantly a combination Hercules-thin man (mesomorph-ectomorph) type. Likewise, the longer the race, the shorter in height are the winners. The trackmen specializing in the 400 meter distance will be approximately four to five inches taller than the winners of the 5,000 to 10,000 meter events. The individuals at this track meet who are predominantly en-

INTRODUCTION

domorphs or spherical persons (heavy, round head, rounded body, and more fat) will be almost entirely among the spectators.

In other words, the use of this concept of body types is useful in predicting athletic careers. If your son, who is five feet nine inches in height, wins All-State honors as a high school quarterback and four years later is selected as the quarterback for the All-American team in college even though he is only five-ten at graduation, he should not expect to be a quarterback in professional football.

The use of types in looking at churches also can be helpful in both analysis and prediction. Victims of heart attacks usually display several common characteristics. This lists includes stress, ancestors with a history of heart attacks, obesity, inadequate exercise, smoking, high blood pressure, excessive use of alcoholic beverages, a high cholesterol count and diabetes. Very few heart attack victims have every one of these characteristics, but nearly every victim of a heart attack has at least four.

Similarly it is possible to identify at least some of the characteristics common to different types of congregations. Rarely will one find a congregation which possesses every characteristic on the list, but most congregations of that type will reflect most of those characteristics for that type. In classifying churches by type it should be remembered that congregations, like people, usually turn out to be a combination of two or three different types. Again some churches, as is also true with people, will reflect to the same degree the characteristics of three different types, but most people and most congregations are predominantly of one type.

After a congregation has been categorized by type, it often is possible to carry out a more creative diagnosis of the situation and to consider alternative prescriptions. Hopefully this process of analysis and diagnosis will help people move away from the tendency toward either scapegoating or hero worship ("We never had these kinds of problems when Dr. Adams was our pastor.") which are both signs of immaturity and toward the more mature approach of accepting both the strengths and limitations of people and of institutions which are governed by mere mortals.

This book was completed at a time when the tendency toward scapegoating may have reached a peak. Examples include the increased publicity about demonology, the renewed interest in exorcism, the speculation by a former army general that "some sinister force" had caused an eighteen-minute erasure in a presidential tape, the reaction to high food prices, the response to the energy crisis, a vice-presidential statement which placed the blame for the Watergate fiasco on "an arrogant, elite guard of political adolescents," and a new wave of anti-Semitism.

Another value in looking at churches by types is that organizations do have a profound impact on the behavior patterns of individuals. The difference in the behavior patterns between two ordained ministers probably will be due in part to differences between the two individuals in terms of personality, values, attitudes, social class backgrounds, amount and type of formal education, early toilet training, and age. Perhaps of even greater importance, however, in understanding these differences among ministers is the impact of the organization on the minister. The expectations placed on the pastor often vary greatly from one type of congregation to another, even within the same denomination. This point is illustrated by the dilemma of the pastor which was described a few pages earlier. The impact of the organization on the behavior patterns of a minister also is illustrated by many ministers when they leave the pastorate to take a position in the denominational bureaucracy.

The same basic point is illustrated as well by the changes in the behavior pattern of the lay person who moves from a relatively passive follower role to an active and demanding leadership role in that same congregation for several years and then back to a passive follower role. A common approach to this pattern is to ask, "What's happened to George? When he was on the Board, I saw him around the church two or three times a week. Now I only see him once every couple of months."

What happens to George when he moves away from the community in which he is an active leader in one type congregation and transfers his membership to a new congregation in the same denomination but of a radically different type? Is this one reason why a move to a different community is one of the three major occasions when church members "drop out" of an active role in the life of the worshiping congregation? (The other two major drop-out points are graduation from high school and soon after the youngest child leaves home.)

In his recent book, *Political Organizations*, James Q. Wilson has suggested that "Finding and explaining uniformities, both trivial and important, is the special competence, and perhaps the chief function of social science." (New York: Basic Books, Inc., 1973). This quotation offers a relevant introduction to a brief description of the contents of this volume. The first chapter suggests a frame of reference for examining three issues which cut across the lines dividing congregations by types. These three subjects come up time after time in parish planning in most congregations regardless of age, location, or type.

The next six chapters describe six different types of congregations. Each chapter is devoted to one of the more common types of churches. The basic approach is to begin with a brief description of one or more kinds of congregations followed by a summary of the more common characteristics of its type and to close with prescriptive comments which may be of help to leaders as they plan for ministry today and tomorrow.

Readers who would like to pursue this approach to church planning and seek descriptive statements of other types of congregation are encouraged to turn to the fifty-page sixth chapter of *Parish Planning* (Nashville: Abingdon Press, 1971).

The eighth chapter is related to the six previous chapters in general and to the seventh chapter in particular. In this chapter an attempt has been made to describe the distinctive characteristics of the contemporary church. Those who seek a conceptual handle for the congregation which is forced to redefine its role before it can begin to plan for today and tomorrow may find the ninth chapter to be of assistance. This chapter begins with a brief description of five different types of congregations caught in an identity crisis and concludes with both general and specific suggestions on responding to this issue.

The last chapter is intended to be a transition between the reading of a book and the practice of church planning. For nearly all congregations faced with the necessity of moving from an emphasis on survival goals to a redefinition of role—and also for a substantial proportion of all other types of churches—this may be the logical beginning point in planning for the future.

During the past fifteen years I have had the enviable opportunity of visiting a total of approximately three thousand congregations in forty states and three nations. Many of these visits are for only an hour or two or perhaps a long evening session with a leadership group. Others are for a full day and an evening, while every year twenty to thirty of these visits are two, three, or four-day in-depth consultations with a single congregation. The material in this volume is drawn from these visits which annually provide firsthand contacts, interviews, and discussions with approximately three thousand people in congregations from a score or more denominations.

While it may be tempting, it would be inconsiderate,

illegal, irresponsible, unethical, and contrary to a major thesis of this book to attempt to place on others the responsibility for errors of fact, analysis, or interpretation which may be scattered through this volume. That responsibility must rest on the shoulders of the author.

It also is impossible to thank by name the hundreds of dedicated church members, both lay and clergy, who have helped write this book. There are, however, a dozen to whom I am especially indebted for their insights, intellectual stimulation, and assistance. This list includes Ron Cochran, Gerald Jones, Mike Murray, John Parks, Leon Phillips, Dave Quill, George Reeves, Mel Sterba, Walter Welch, Charles Lee Wilson, Rip Winkler, and Lloyd Wright.

This volume is dedicated to two wonderful people who continually radiate to everyone around them the finest of the virtues of the committed Christian including faith in God, a love of Christ, a profound neighbor-centered concern, a wholesome respect for God's creation, and a never-failing cheerfulness, humility, patience, hope, and wry sense of good humor. All of us who have been blessed by knowing them are in their debt.

1
Community, Commitment, and Birthdates

The most overused and least productive tool in church planning is a map. A widely used practice is to secure a street map of an area, indicate the locations of the meeting places of all of the religious congregations on this map, and draw a circle with a radius equal to one mile around the symbol marking the location of each building.

Another common practice is to use a larger map, mark with an appropriate symbol the meeting places of all the congregations of a single denomination in the geographical area included on that map, and draw a series of large circles around several clusters of church buildings.

Both practices share a common hazard. Once the map has been prepared and is shown to people, it is very tempting to refer to the map and to develop solutions to complex parish planning problems on the basis of the information symbolized by the marks and lines on the map. What is often overlooked is that the information reflected by the maps may be comparatively insignificant while more significant data is neglected. In other words, maps tempt people to try to develop simple solutions to complex problems in parish planning—and simplistic answers to complex problems often are counterproductive! If the maps did not exist, it would increase the chances that the people involved would seek more abstract, subjective, and useful information in analyzing the problem and looking at alternative courses of action.

To state it more bluntly, the presence of these maps

with the precisely located symbols and the carefully drawn circles often tempt people to believe they have enough data for analyzing a problem, but this reliance on maps often obscures the need for information more difficult to obtain. This reliance on maps may cause people to believe they have all the information they need rather than to cause them to be apprehensive about the omission of other more helpful data.

This temptation to rely on easily obtainable information, rather than to seek less accessible but more revealing data, can be illustrated in another way. Perhaps the four most widely reported numbers by congregations in American Protestantism are number of members, Sunday school enrollment, Sunday school attendance, and annual dollar receipts. Far more useful, however, in any attempt to describe comtemporary reality would be the answers to these four questions: (1) What was the average attendance at Sunday morning worship for the past twelve months? (2) How many groups are there in the congregation in which most of the members of that group find membership to be very meaningful? (3) What proportion of the *resident confirmed* members are members of these groups? (4) What proportion of the member-households accounted for 50 percent of the dollar receipts from the membership last year?

The central thesis of this book is that it often is more helpful to turn away from the maps and membership figures and to focus greater attention on looking at churches by type. Several of the more common types of churches are discussed in the remaining chapters of this volume. The basic purpose of this introductory chapter is to look at three of the most significant considerations in church planning. All three are useful in looking at congregations by types. In effect, they are cross-categories which overlap the types of churches described later. All three also are among the most neglected or misunderstood concepts in church planning.

What Is Community?

"We must minister to this community in which our church is located, but where do we begin and how do we do it?" This question frequently comes up as congregational leaders look at a map showing the location of the meeting place of that congregation. The map may have a series of concentric circles drawn around the location of the building, with the radius of the smallest circle representing a distance of one-half mile from the congregational meeting place and the radius of the largest circle representing a distance of five or ten or twenty miles. If the members are represented by dots on the map, it is not uncommon to encounter a situation in which two-thirds of these dots are located at a distance of three miles or more from the church building.

In responding to this question it may be helpful to ask two sets of questions. First, what is meant by "church"? Does that word refer to the community often identified by the word "congregation"? Or does that word refer to the body of Christ? Or does it simply refer to the building which is the meeting place of this congregation? This is a very basic theological and biblical issue!

Second, what is meant by "community"? A geographically defined area on the map? A group of people who can be defined by social, economic, educational, nationality, language, racial, age, theological, cultural, and life-style characteristics? What is the referent in the question for the word "this" and for the word "our"?

Recently these questions about the nature of community were lifted up to greater visibility with the publication of a book bemoaning the loss of community. Written by the well-known social critic, Vance Packard, this provocative best seller, *A Nation of Strangers*,[1] has caught the attention of many church leaders.

[1] New York: Pocket Books, 1972.

22

There are at least two reasons why church leaders should take Packard's latest book seriously. The more important of these is that the diagnosis of American society, the assorted statistics, and the conclusions of the book will be quoted widely by leaders in the churches as they attempt to define the role and the ministries of the churches in the seventies. Sometimes these will be misquotations and sometimes the quote will be what Packard has written, but what he wrote does not always accurately reflect reality.

For example, on page 19 is the sentence, "According to one estimate, about 10,000 salespeople leave Charlotte every Monday morning to make the rounds of branch or local offices." Recently this was quoted as "Vance Packard says that every Monday morning 50,000 traveling salesmen leave Charlotte and they're away from home all week." These are very interesting numbers since the 1970 census of Charlotte reported (1) only 10,945 salespersons employed in the Charlotte labor force and 4,507 of these were in retail trade; (2) there were only 17,056 sales workers living in the entire two-county Charlotte metropolitan area, of whom 7,029 were in retail sales, and (3) including all occupations less than seven thousand of all the 153,179 persons in the entire labor force of Mecklenburg County, of which Charlotte is the hub, travel across a county line when they go to work.

The second reason this book deserves the serious attention of church leaders is that Packard speaks clearly to those who "want our church to serve this community" and for those who want to turn the clock back to yesterday.

Packard's basic contention is that the sense of community is disappearing, and he claims that already forty million Americans lead rootless lives. He identifies five forms of "uprooting," the first of which is the repeated moves of so many families. The second is the disruption of many authentic communities as a result of such factors as urban growth sprawling

23

out over previously stable rural communities, urban renewal, highway clearance projects, and the general decentralization of the urban population. The third is the increasing anonymity of urban life with many people unacquainted with their neighbors across the street or in an adjoining apartment. The fourth is the impact on a sense of community when neighbors work different shifts at an around-the-clock factory, store or business. Finally, Packard points to the fragmentation of the family as another factor in the growing rootlessness of the American population.

This book will be useful reading for church members who are torn by a sense of guilt because their church is not "serving the community." One of the major indirect contributions that comes from Packard's research is that it is deceptive to think in terms of a geographical area, such as a dozen city blocks, as automatically constituting a "community" or even a "neighborhood."

A growing body of research indicates that an increasing proportion of Americans do not "neighbor" with the people living next door or down the street. Instead, most Americans continue to socialize primarily with kinfolk, with people who work in the same occupation or profession or in the same department or on the same shift, with people from the same socioeconomic class, with persons who are members of the same church, and with people from the same nationality, race, or cultural background. This pattern is much the same as it was fifty or one hundred years ago. The major differences are (1) these groupings do not coincide with the identification of a geographically defined community to the same degree as was true in 1880 or 1930, (2) sons do not tend to follow in the vocational footsteps of their fathers as they once did, and (3) members of family groupings are more scattered, thus more travel is required for visits with kinfolk although improved travel facilities make this easier. A hundred years ago, or even fifty years ago, it was not unusual for brothers and sisters not to see one another for three or four decades or longer. In 1910 or 1920 it was not uncommon for a youngster to grow up without even knowing the names of all his aunts and uncles, much less seeing them occasionally.

In simple language what this means is that "the community" with which a person is identified seldom can be defined meaningfully only in geographical terms. One result is that the religious congregation that wants to serve its community has a more difficult task of defining that community. It will probably produce frustration for the urban church to define it in geographical terms. For the rural church to ignore economic, social, cultural, educational, racial, and ethnic considerations also probably will produce frustration. The churches seeking to bring the gospel of Jesus Christ to persons outside their own membership tend to be more effective when they define community in terms of people and the characteristics of people rather than in geographical terms.

Which offers the best handles for developing a ministry to people beyond the membership of the congregation? To say, "Our emphasis is on a ministry to everyone living within six blocks of the church" or to say, "Our special emphasis is ministry is to alienated street kids," or "to older widowed women living alone," or "to unmarried pregnant high school girls," or "to parents whose youngest child is about to leave home." Which alternative suggests that the people defining their evangelistic outreach have thought through what they are seeking to do?

Vance Packard, like many other Americans in their fifties, is an ex-farm boy who has made good in a highly specialized vocation that was not available to people living in rural America in the years following World War II. This brings us to the heart of an evaluation of the basic theme of the book, the gradual disappearance of some of the ties that bound people which could be visualized and described in geographical terms. Many of us regret the passing of the day when it was easy for the children to run next door and visit Grandma, or when three hundred relatives and friends gathered for the funeral of a local resident, or when a person worked for the same employer and retired after forty years of faithful service and was given a gold watch. These are the days and the conditions which constitute the ideal as the continuing thread in Packard's narrative.

In the United States we have traded off the benefits of community which could be defined in geographical terms for such benefits as greater vocational mobility across generation lines, for increased freedom of choice in employment, housing, friends, climate, and schools, and for a much less paternalistic economic environment. The black son of a sharecropper in the South, by moving to Chicago or Detroit or Cleveland or New York, traded off the opportunity to follow in his father's footsteps as a sharecropper for the opportunity to be a janitor or teacher or postal worker or garbage collector or drug pusher or congressman or welfare recipient. Has it been a good trade? That is the basic question. The alternative of having both the benefits of a geographically defined community and the benefits that require residential and vocational mobility does not appear to be on the list of options today.

The Test in the Marketplace

The question of whether it was a good trade is subjective and difficult to answer. One of the best places to seek an answer is in the marketplace. Widespread national publicity has been given to the new towns of Reston and Columbia as exciting and successful examples of how small-town life, intimacy, and sense of community can be recaptured. The public relations materials that form the basis for so many of these literary accolades are contradicted by experience. Reston turned out to be an economic failure. The design won architectural awards, but prospective home buyers came, looked, and bought elsewhere. The attractive village center on the lake became the focal point for the distribution of drugs. In Columbia, the research of John B. Slidell documented what Suzanne Keller reported in *The Urban Neighborhood.*[2] The neighborhood unit reflects the dreams of planners rather than the expressed wants and needs of people. People tend "to neighbor" along existing friendship, kinship, educational, vocational, cultural, racial, ethnic, and religious lines rather than within a geographically defined neighborhood. One result is that the church planning in Columbia which produced one large meeting place for several "village" congregations, probably will not be duplicated in other new towns. In Columbia, as elsewhere, people attend the church of their choice, which may or may not be the one meeting in a building located near their residence. A majority of the churchgoers leave Columbia to attend church.

Perhaps next to new towns the most widely publicized approach to the "new" community of the future has been the shopping center mall. A few, such as the Monroeville Mall in suburban Pittsburgh, have placed a major emphasis on community relations, but that is far different than building a sense of community! The shopping center owners, like the developers of new towns, often find a conflict between building community and economic pressures. The latter always win, sooner or later.

While it is far more difficult reading, the churchman who is interested in a serious study of mobility should turn not to *A Nation of Strangers* but to *People of the United States in the 20th Century* by Irene B. and Conrad Taeuber.[3] This thousand-page research

[2] New York: Random House, 1968.
[3] Bureau of the Census, 1971.

monograph points out that in 1960 there were 159 million persons aged five and over in the United States. Almost exactly one-half (79 million) lived in the same house as they occupied in 1955. In 1970 the number of persons age five and over had climbed to 186 million, but a slightly larger proportion, or 54 percent (98.5 million), lived in the same house they had occupied five years earlier.

In any given year, approximately 81 percent of the population (exclusive of armed forces personnel) do not move, 12 percent move to another address within the county, 3 percent move to a different county within the state, and 4 percent move to a different state. These percentages have dropped slightly in recent years, but basically they have been the same for at least a quarter of a century. Nearly one-half the moves each year are made by persons either under five years of age or in the seventeen-to-thirty age bracket.

If one shifts to a longer time span, three generalizations stand out from the census data. First, in any five-year period approximately one-half of the population accounts for that often quoted figure that one-fifth of the population move every year. Second, well over one-fourth of the people stay at the same address for at least ten years (one person in seven had been living at the same address for at least twenty years). Third, for the past hundred years each decennial census has shown that approximately three-fourths of all native-born Americans are living in the state in which they were born. In North Carolina, for example, 83 percent of the American-born residents of 1970 had been born in that state. In Florida that figure was only 37 percent, but in Tennessee it was 74 percent, in Texas 73 percent, and in Pennsylvania 83 percent.

It is easy to make the leap from the generalization that one-fifth of the American people move each year to some statement such as, "That means we must anticipate a 20 percent turnover in our church membership every year." On an overall denominational average, about 6 or 7 percent of the members of any denomination change congregations each year. This figure is approximately the same for Baptists as it is for Lutherans or Methodists or Presbyterians or Episcopalians or Unitarians. One reason is that many church members change their address, but continue their affiliation with the same church since most moves keep the person within driving distance of his home church. A second reason is that church members tend to be drawn from those segments of the population that are less mobile.

It is easy to overstate the degree of mobility in the American population, as Vance Packard and so many others have done in writing on the subject, or in the church, as many leaders do, and to identify the mobility of the population as the cause of many problems. A more helpful frame of reference is to conceptualize the population or membership as being divided into two groups. Approximately one-half of the people belong in one group. These are the ones who change their place of residence infrequently, no more often than once every seven years on the average. Many have been living in the same house for one or two or three decades or longer. The second and smaller group is composed of those people who move more frequently, and some of them change their address two or three times a year.

It is worth returning briefly to Vance Packard's book in order to lift up three insights and ideas that can be useful in helping a church identify and implement its ministry more adequately. Repeatedly Packard emphasizes the value for newcomers to a community to "rebuild their social circle." He is supportive of intentional and systematic efforts to help the newcomers become accepted in their new neighborhood as neighbors. He writes, "Churches play an important role here. Don't just go to church. The old friendliness

29

of earlier decades when after the services everyone chatted with people in nearby pews has disappeared in many areas. . . . To become integrated you need to become an *active* churchgoer. . . . The church is only one organization that offers instant involvement."

This is a relevant point. Many newcomers to a community do actively seek out the church as they begin to put down new roots. Some churches are active in contacting newcomers and encouraging instant involvement while others appear to say: "The door is always open. If they want to develop a new church relationship after moving, we expect them to take the initiative."

A second point which Packard makes indirectly in a negative manner is the importance of being careful of impressionistic responses to complex questions. For example, are frequent moves harmful to children? Packard devotes an entire chapter to this question. One nine-line paragraph reviews briefly some of the research that indicates high mobility has no negative impact on I.Q. or school grades or personal adjustment and suggests that while the differences are minor, the children in highly mobile families may have an advantage over those who live in the same house for ten or fifteen years. The other nine pages are devoted to the contention that while there are neither facts nor research to support this point, frequent moves must be bad for children. Too often decision-making in the churches follows the same pattern. The facts all point in one direction, but we follow our hunches and move in the other direction. Packard would have profited from reading *Urban Dynamics* by Jay W. Forrester,[4] who declared, after detailed research on efforts to solve contemporary social problems, that in complex social systems "intuitively sensible policies can affect adversely the very problems they are designed to alleviate."

[4] Cambridge, Mass.: M.I.T. Press, 1969.

Finally, scattered through the book are several thought-provoking phrases and sentences that stick with the reader. Two can be cited to illustrate this. One is Packard's contention that unlike a hundred years ago, the highly mobile people are the "winners" in society rather than the "losers." Any minister reading that may want to reflect on it, on himself, and on his colleagues. It may or may not be an accurate broad generalization. Another is Packard's contention that "there is a general shattering of small-group life." This suggests one approach the churches can use in reaching and ministering to newcomers. This generalization also supports the value of the second and third of the four questions suggested on page 12 of this chapter. The churches that have placed a major emphasis on creating new opportunities for personal and spiritual growth through small groups usually find this a creative approach not only for lonely newcomers, but also for longtime residents.

Thus, one answer for the church leaders who ask the question, "How can we serve this community?" may be simply, "Create a sense of community."

The Generational Gap

One of the oldest sociological principles is that the individual is influenced by the era in which he or she grew from childhood into adulthood.[5] This also is one of the most neglected considerations in church planning. Too often the median age of the congregation is considered in terms of the probable life expectancy of that religious institution rather than as a major factor in the decision-making process. Thus the congregation in which most of the adults are in the 30-40 age bracket is perceived as having "a great future" while the one in which most of the adults have passed their

[5] For another discussion of this point see Lyle E. Schaller, *The Decision-Makers* (Nashville: Abingdon Press, 1973), pp. 48-50.

sixtieth birthday is seen as having "a very limited future unless they begin to reach young married couples." This heretical and institution-oriented view totally neglects the New Testament imperative for ministry *now*.

In addition, it is a diversionary approach to effective planning. This can be illustrated by a quick visit to several congregations. In the church school wing of the first congregation the chairs in every room are set up in rows facing a desk at one end of the room. In the church school wing of the second congregation the chairs in every one of the twelve rooms are arranged in a circle. When were the church school superintendent and teacher in the first congregation born? In the second?

In the third congregation an adult Sunday school class is split over planning for next year. One group wants to select a person who will have the responsibility to teach the lessons from the denominational quarterly. The other group wants to bring in a series of guest speakes who will lead discussions on Christianity and contemporary issues. When were most of the members of the first group born? Of the second group?

In a fourth congregation the vote at the annual meeting was 69 to 61 to terminate the lease with the city recreation department for use of the fellowship hall and gymnasium as the meeting place for the municipally financed youth program. What was the median age of those on the prevailing side of this vote? Of those on the losing side?

In the fifth congregation the church school wing, which was built in 1948, has been completely remodeled and provided with the very finest in furniture and equipment. The rooms for the nursery, for the two-year-olds, for the three- and four-year-olds and for the kindergartners are spotless and in perfect order. They could be photographed and the pictures used in a brochure on the model church school facility. How old are the persons who initiated, planned, financed, and carried through this remodeling?

In the sixth and largest congregation on this visit the person who was called four years ago to serve as the youth minister was dismissed after eighteen months. Recently, two and one-half years later, the congregation instructed the senior pastor and the church council that the number one priority was to find a minister "who can build a good youth program" and thus reverse the recent trend which now finds the high school youth group composed of six girls and two boys. What proportion of those voting to make this the high priority have children under eighteen years of age?

In each of these six congregations the planning and decision-making processes involved cross-generational considerations, but the resulting differences were largely overlooked. In the third, fourth, and sixth congregations one result was internal conflict while in the first, second, fifth, and sixth, one result was frustration.

While it is a misleading oversimplification to suggest that everyone born between 1915 and 1928 speaks from the same perspective and holds to the same value system, it is even more frustrating to ignore the generational concept and the impact of the formative years on an individual's values, expectations, attitudes, and behavior patterns. Perhaps the best contemporary illustration of the value of the generational concept is that in nearly every religious organization one of the most pressing issues is how to involve the people born after 1945 in identifying and planning the churches' responses to the religious needs of those whom Margaret Mead has labeled "The Oldest Postwar People."[6]

In most of the types of congregations discussed in subsequent chapters the frustration produced by the

[6] Margaret Mead, "The Oldest Postwar People," *New York Times*, 21 January, 1973.

efforts of one generation to identify and respond to the religious needs of a younger generation is a common thread.

Commitment and Assimilation

At the fiftieth anniversary celebration of the founding of a midwestern Swedish Lutheran congregation a charter member had been asked to speak and to describe the changes he had witnessed since that day, five decades earlier, when a small band of Swedish immigrants had gathered to form the original nucleus of this parish. He began his remarks by reading the names from a list of recent new members. "Androwitz, Buchanan, Kanokis, Makino, McCauley, Vitale. . . ," he read. Then he looked puzzled and asked, "So what kind of Sveds are these?"

While those present responded with a good-natured laugh to his puzzled expression, this charter member was illustrating another important dimension of church planning. What is the commitment of the various members to *this* congregation? How deep is that commitment? Why are some members more committed to the life, ministry, and goals of *this* congregation than others? How can we help new members deepen their commitment to *this* congregation? Again these questions form a recurring thread which runs through most types of congregations.

One approach to these questions is to look at commitment in a manner which runs counter to biblical and theological ideals, but which does reflect a portion of contemporary reality. There are people who are committed to Jesus Christ as Lord and Savior, but who are not active and participating members of any worshiping congregation. There are others also committed to Jesus Christ as Lord and Savior who find membership in a worshiping congregation to be essential for fulfilling, expressing, and nurturing that commitment.

In most congregations it is possible to divide the adult membership into four categories. First, there are those who have long and deep roots in this congregation. These roots may run back through two or three generations or they may have been acquired through birth or marriage. These are the people who have a commitment to *this* congregation based primarily on shared roots, on past experiences, and on a common heritage.

Second, there are the members who have a strong commitment to *this* congregation because of what it is doing in ministry and program *now*. This may be in the form of a ministry *to* that member or that member's family. It may be in the form of enabling that member to be directly involved in ministry through this congregation. It may be in the form of an outreach ministry which wins the vigorous support, although not the active involvement, of this member. Whatever the form, this member's commitment to this congregation is based on contemporary goals and program, not on the past or on heritage.

Third, there may be members who have a strong commitment to *this* congregation based on *both* heritage and contemporary goals.

Fourth, there may be persons who have their names on the membership roll, but have neither a heritage nor a contemporary goals tie to *this* congregation. Most of these people are comparatively or totally inactive members.

Now, what does this say to the assimilation of new members into the ongoing life, fellowship, and ministry of the worshiping congregation?

First, the "heritage" type congregation may have difficulty reaching and assimilating persons other than those who are born or marry into this congregation.

Second, the contemporary goals of today quickly are converted into a heritage from the past. A representative illustration of this is the new mission founded in 1952 which was deeply involved in major building programs in 1954, 1958, and 1966. One-half of today's members have joined since 1967, but none of them were involved in the unifying, highly visible, and tangible goals represented by the three building programs. Why is it that while one-half of the pre-1967 members attend Sunday morning worship at least twice a month, only one-fourth of the persons joining since 1967 attend at least twice a month? Why is it that 85 percent of all leaders in this congregation joined before 1966? Should the last building program, which was also the largest, be viewed as a contemporary goal of the mid-1960s, but as a part of the heritage when viewed from the mid-1970s?

Third, the congregation with a large proportion of its membership in the "heritage" category usually either (1) will have difficulty reaching and assimilating new members or (2) will develop its contemporary goals in a manner which facilitates the assimilation of newcomers.

Fourth, the division between the "heritage" members and the "contemporary goals" members often is a major source of internal conflict. This division often is widened by the generational gap described in the previous section.

Finally, the fastest growing congregations in American Christianity tend to be those which have two common characteristics. The first is a clear self-image or identity (see chapter ten for an elaboration of this point). The second common characteristic is a series of contemporary goals which also provide opportunities for the assimilation of new members.

Another approach to this issue of the assimilation of new members can be described by the term "points of entry." What are the points of entry for new members into the life, fellowship, and ministry of the typical parish? One approach is to look at a typical congregation in the manner described by this diagram. The box represents the entire congregation.

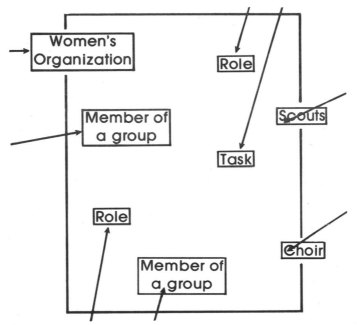

Each arrow represents one individual joining that congregation. Some individuals join and assume a "role" (Sunday school teacher, Scoutmaster, treasurer, usher, trustee, etc.) and are assimilated into the life and fellowship through that route.

Other individuals join the congregation and become members of a group in which membership is especially meaningful to the members. These groups include Sunday school classes, circles in the women's organization, study groups, Koinonia groups, short-term study-fellowship groups, and similar clusterings of people in small groups.

A few individuals become a part of some group before they actually become confirmed members of the congregation. The choir, Scouting, and the women's organization are the most common examples of this. Once the adult Sunday school class was a very common example of this pattern.

Some individuals become members and are assimilated into the life and fellowship of the congregation by becoming involved in a task such as planning and carrying out the plans for a bazaar, a building program, a service ministry requiring several volunteers for a specified period of time, a picnic, or some other task. Most other people who join a worshiping congregation and do not fall into one of the above categories become inactive members.

Thus groups, roles, tasks, and organizations serve as *both* a point of entry into the congregation *and* as a means of being assimilated into the life and fellowship of the congregation.

2
The Church on the Plateau

The Maple Grove Church is an eighty-year-old congregation in rural community. The white frame building is located in the open country on a blacktop county highway.

For the past few decades the reported membership figure has fluctuated between 35 and 50 and every Sunday finds approximately 35 people gathered for worship. The worship attendance has held steady at about 35 as far back as anyone can remember—and no one expects it to climb or decline in the foreseeable future.

Bethel Church was started as a mission in the new church development boom of the early 1960s. The first worship was held in January, 1961, with a total attendance of 56 persons. The charter membership roll was closed the following November with 73 members.

Housing construction moved at a slower rate than had been anticipated when the new mission was launched, and the membership total rose very slowly. A $93,000 multipurpose meeting place was completed in early 1965, and that produced an $80,000 mortgage with monthly payments of $830.

When the first pastor left a year later, the resident membership total stood at 140; worship attendance averaged between 70 and 80, receipts from the membership averaged slightly less than $1,800 monthly, and the Sunday church school attendance had leveled off at 45.

In an effort to balance a severely strained budget, catch up on overdue mortgage payments, and "face reality," the leaders at Bethel decided not to replace the departing pastor with a full-time minister. An arrangement was worked out with the 160-member Trinity Church eight miles away whereby these two struggling congregations would share a pastor.

Since this minister and his family moved into the relatively new Bethel parsonage, the Bethel congregation paid only $4,500 of the $11,000 cash "compensation package" (cash salary, utilities, travel, pension, and health insurance) received by the new minister. This arrangement relieved the severe financial pressure which had been on the people at Bethel.

In 1973 worship attendance averaged 76, receipts from members totaled $21,900, and the members were looking forward to 1976 when the mortgage would be retired and they could begin to think about actually starting the long-discussed and twice-delayed second building program.

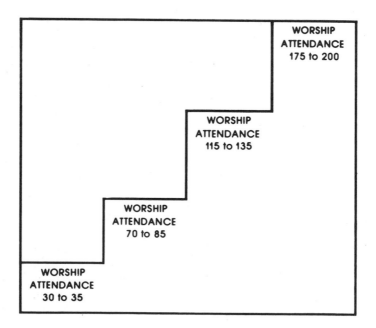

THE CHURCH ON THE PLATEAU

The Elmwood Church was established in 1883 on the edge of what then was a small rural community. The membership total did not reach 100 until the mid-1950s when the growing exodus of people from the adjacent large metropolitan center transformed Elmwood from a sleepy rural community into part of exurbia.

As the population of the community increased the membership of the church climbed. When it passed the 200 mark in 1959, the congregation went ahead with a proposal to build a U-shaped fellowship hall-educational unit on the wooded five-acre site behind the 70-year-old frame structure that was set back only twelve feet from the highway.

The plans called for use of the old building as a worship center for five or six years. At that time it was hoped the congregation would be large enough and the mortgage small enough to go ahead with construction of a new worship facility.

In 1966 the old building was torn down, partly because the alternative would have been to invest at least $9,000 in a new heating system and general remodeling necessary to meet the building code, and partly in the hope that razing the old structure would "force" people to see the need to go ahead with the plan to start a new building program.

Worship attendance at the Elmwood Church peaked at 135 in 1965 and has been on a plateau ever since, fluctuating between an annual average of 126 in 1969 and the high of 133 in 1974.

Today the attendance averages 130, receipts from the members total $32,000 annually, and the debt has been reduced to $47,000. It was refinanced last year and monthly payments are now $500 a month.

The people feel cramped for program space since the old building has been demolished. They are too pessimistic about the future to go ahead with a new building program, but they feel they cannot grow without additional space.

Calvary Church was established in 1951. Today it includes 490 confirmed members, the worship attendance averages 185 to 200 on Sunday morning, the Sunday church school averages 135 to 150, but another 30 to 60 people are involved in short-term educational ventures during the week.

In a typical year at least 240 different persons will be involved in either a Sunday morning or a weekday study group or class, and last year that figure topped the 300 mark for the first time.

Originally the plans called for a three-phase building program at Calvary with a 350-seat sanctuary in phase three. This plan has been scrapped, however, and the fellowship hall, which was to be only a temporary worship facility, is now seen as the permanent place for worship. It seats 220 comfortably, and with an attendance of 85 at the first service and 100 to 135 at the second, it is not crowded.

The receipts from the members average $48,000 a year including debt service payments of $9,000 on the $58,000 mortgage which covers the remaining indebtedness on both the second building program and the nine-year-old parsonage.

The staff includes a full-time minister, a half-time secretary, a 20-hour-a-week custodian, a $500-a-year choir director, and a $300-a-year organist. Last month the church council decided not to participate in the proposed United Christian Cooperative Ministry which is a proposal to bring together in one cooperative ministry seven congregations. Two of the seven churches are much larger than Calvary while the other four are significantly smaller.

Four Plateaus

These four congregations are typical examples of "the church on a plateau."

There is a tendency to think of the growth (and the decline) of a congregation as resembling a smooth curve. Another way to look at it is to see the growth, or the decline, of a church as resembling a series of stairsteps, with each step as a plateau. There is a tendency for congregations to cluster around several points that can be described as steps or plateaus.

The first of these clusters is the congregation that is on a plateau where worship attendance averages 30 to 35 on Sunday morning. The Maple Grove Church, described earlier in the opening paragraph of this chapter, is one example of a church on this plateau.

The churches on this plateau tend to have several characteristics in common. The most distinctive is that these small congregations tend to function as meaningful groups. Instead of being a congregation composed of several groups, the worshiping congregation itself is one large group and this group is heavily dependent on each member.

Whenever one of the "regulars" is not present for Sunday morning worship, he or she is missed by everyone present. Most of the adults present can easily recall who was at worship last Sunday. If a member who is seldom present for worship does appear, that member is welcomed profusely.

A second characteristic of the church on this plateau is that it is "tough." It holds to life with great tenacity.

It also usually is a very "thrifty" organization and there is little waste in the expenditure of scarce financial resources. There also is a very heavy reliance on volunteers.

Ministers come and go and rarely have any major impact on the life, value system, or orientation of this tightly knit group. This plateau accounts for perhaps 15 percent of all churches in American Protestantism.

———•———

The second plateau is occupied by congregations which typically average 70 to 85 at Sunday morning worship. Many of these are small rural congregations which are limited in potential growth by being in communities where the population is decreasing in numbers.

Some of them are "arrested development" new missions founded in the 1950–1967 era which grew, reached this plateau, leveled off, trimmed their output to match the input of resources, and have remained on this plateau for years, much to the distress of those who helped launch the new mission. Bethel Church referred to earlier is an example of this type of church.

Approximately 10 percent of all congregations in American Protestantism are on this plateau, which can be described as the "survival level." Churches on this plateau are large enough to provide leaders for all of the essential positions.

These congregations are large enough to mobilize the financial resources necessary for survival, and they are sufficiently large, strong, and prosperous to obtain the services of an ordained minister, frequently on a one-half time or one-third time basis.

A substantial number are able to find a pastor who does not serve any other congregation. He may have part-time secular employment or be in school or serve in some nonparochial position in the church such as a chaplain or a campus minister.

————•————

Clustered together on the third step of this series of plateaus are another 5 to 10 percent of the churches. These congregations have a worship attendance which has leveled off at 115 to 135 on the typical Sunday. Some of them are rural-turned-suburban or exurban congregations such as the Elmwood Church described earlier. Others are the product of a merger back in the 1950s or early 1960s which produced a burst of growth and then leveled off.

A few churches of this size are drawn from the ranks of new missions founded in the 1950s or 1960s which have not quite reached the "potential" that was predicted. Others are congregations that were on a higher plateau, in terms of worship attendance, only a few years ago, but have now slipped down to this plateau and appear to have leveled off in terms of size or growth.

The churches on this third step have three common characteristics. First, many were deeply involved in a building program a few years ago. At that time enthusiasm ran high and there was a broad base of participation in planning and implementing this goal. The shift from a highly visible and tangible goal of building to the intangible and less visible goals of ministry have left these congregations without the psychic rewards and satisfactions which earlier helped build enthusiasm and motivate people.

Second, most of these congregations take on many of the attributes of a full-size congregation—with some frustration for both the pastor and the lay leaders. They are not able to "keep up" with the congregations that are averaging 150 or more at worship.

The minister usually is a full-time seminary graduate and frequently under forty years of age. He may feel both frustrated and inadequate as the congregation often is not quite able to accomplish what he believes should be possible in a church with a full-time pastor. Or, he may project impossible goals for the congregation and thus leave the members feeling inadequate and guilty.

The third common characteristic is that many of the congregations on this plateau are somewhat depressed psychologically and spiritually by a combination of (1) the "post-building blues," (2) a debt that makes servicing the mortgage a major element of the purpose of that congregation and (3) a decline in the quality of the group life of the congregation (and often in the number of meaningful groups). This is a

result of the diversion of time and energy to the building (planning-construction-financing) efforts which
usurped the agenda for several years.

On the fourth step of this series of plateaus is the
church with an average attendance at worship of 175
to 200. Most of the congregations that fall into this
category—and they account for another 5 to 10 percent of all the congregations in American
Protestantism—are institutionally "comfortable."

Each one has enough resources (time and energy
of volunteers and money) to carry out a full-scale
church program, but not enough to spare that the
leaders feel they can risk sharing any with other ventures via a cooperative ministry.

This type of congregation usually is sufficiently
large and complex to keep a full-time minister busy
and also to provide him with the "satisfactions" of a
meaningful and productive ministry.

This type of congregation includes relatively young
congregations which have "leveled off" at this size. It
includes many downtown churches in cities of 5,000
to 50,000 population. It includes a significant number
of "neighborhood churches" which now draw members from a rather large area. It also includes many
strong suburban congregations that have passed
their fiftieth birthday.

It also includes a substantial number of congregations in small towns and even a few that have the
meeting place out in the open country. It includes a
growing number of what formerly were rural churches
that spent several decades on the first or second of
this series of plateaus before the city folks began to
move to the country and helped the congregation
climb to this fourth step.

Limitations to This Concept

There are some important limitations in using this
concept of a church on a plateau.

First, approximately two-thirds of the churches in American Protestantism do not fit anywhere into this frame of reference.

Second, it should be emphasized that this frame of reference is useful only in working with congregations that appear to be relatively stable or that have been on the same step or plateau for several years.

Third, while many churches in a period of institutional decline appear to fit into this concept, there is one very important distinction. The church which is in a period of statistical decline may appear to be dropping in size in a pattern that also resembles a series of stairsteps. It often spends several years on one plateau before dropping down to the next one.

The important distinction, however, is that unlike the churches on the four plateaus described earlier, the congregation on the downward series of steps often has accumulated significant institutional assets. Thus, instead of a mortgage on a new building it may have an endowment fund. Instead of a part-time secretary, as is often the case with the church that has never averaged more than 175 at worship, it often has at least one full-time secretary, despite a worship attendance figure that rarely exceeds 180.

The loyalty and the giving level of members of the congregation on the downward side of the stairs often is greater than on the other side where there is not the recollection of "the good old days" and where there are fewer people who have been members for over forty years. (One of the most influential factors in determining the level of giving in a congregation is the proportion of members who have been members for longer than two decades.) Likewise the pastor of the church on the downward side of the stairsteps frequently is older than the pastor of a similar size congregation which is on the other side of the growth and decline curve. Not infrequently he is less than ten years from retirement.

A fourth limitation of this typology is that the

generalizations which are helpful in working with congregations under 200 in average worship attendance do not prove to be as helpful in working with larger congregations. When a congregation averages over 200 at worship on Sunday morning, a different typology usually will be more helpful in analyzing its situation.

Finally, it must be remembered that this is a useful frame of reference in many, *but not all,* cases. There are congregations on a plateau where it is more helpful to use a different frame of reference in looking at the future. Several of these are described in subsequent chapters.

Lessons From Experience

What can the congregation on a plateau do as it looks ahead toward tomorrow? Will it be on this plateau forever? Is there any way to move up to another step?

While it cannot be emphasized too strongly that each church is different from all others on the same plateau, there are several principles that have proved to be helpful in other congregations that found themselves on a plateau.

1. When possible use a "both-and" approach rather than an "either-or" approach. Avoid change by subtraction or replacement in favor of change by addition. This means plan new programs, new approaches to worship, new groups, new ventures in Christian education, or new avenues of outreach as *additions,* rather than as replacements for existing programs and ministries.

2. Intentionally and systemically plan to broaden the base of ownership of goals (programs). This applies to both old and new programs, to both old and new goals.

3. Keep the agenda focused on the possibilities, opportunities, and potentialities of tomorrow, not on

problems, not on the limitations imposed by yesterday's experiences.

4. Congregations on a plateau tend to look inward and to focus on a ministry to members and their children. Build in an emphasis on ministry to people in the community beyond the membership.

5. Do not "blame" the inactive members for your current situation. You have no control over their behavior. The leaders of your church do have control, however, over what the leaders expect and plan. Therefore, concentrate your planning where the leaders have control, not where they have no control.

6. Periodically monitor the program to determine if people actually are being given real choices. Too often a church offers only a very limited range of program choices to people and, therefore, many persons select one choice and stick with it. That choice is to stay away.

7. Resist the tendency to think in terms of a congregational frame of reference. This is reductionism. Most congregations are, in fact, congregations of groups of people. Even in the small congregations it often is helpful to think, plan, and program for groups of people rather than for the entire congregation as if it were only one group.

How many groups are there in which membership in that group is meaningful to the members? How long ago was the newest group formed? How many members are a part of at least one group? How many groups are really open to new members? To the inactive members?

8. Keep working at efforts to broaden the tolerance base. In most congregations that have been on the same plateau for any length of time there is a tendency to stick with "That's how we've always done it here." Encourage people to at least tolerate, if not accept, that which they may find to be new, different, unusual, strange, or innovative.

9. Many of the churches on a plateau are filled with

low expectations, excessive pessimism, and negative attitudes. Often this is at least in part a response to a lack of knowledge of what is happening in and through the life and ministry of that worshiping congregation.

One approach to this situation is to lift up for celebration in a special worship experience once or twice a year all that has happened during the preceding several months.

Another related and compatible approach is to use the goal setting process as a means of reporting back to the congregation *on a regular basis* what is planned and what is happening as the congregation moves toward these goals.

Use of a five-year planning cycle is another means of raising the level of expectations. The development of a three-, four-, or five-year plan tends to raise expectations *and* to provide a systematic approach for implementing those expectations.

10. Ask yourselves, "What is our specialty?" Many congregations find new life and enthusiasm by developing one or two forms of specialized ministry *in addition* to the traditional package of programs and ministries.

What are the areas of potential specialization for your church? A ministry to visually handicapped persons? To young married couples with their first child? To the drug scene? To widowed women? To high school girls? To newcomers in this neighborhood?

11. Finally, look carefully at what is, in fact, the purpose of your church. Do not listen to the clichés, but examine the actions of the congregation. Is the real purpose to pay off the mortgage? To keep this institution going? To recruit new workers to replace persons who become old and tired? To glorify God? To serve Christ? To help people? To be a reconciling force in a fragmented world?

A review of the actual purpose may be the beginning point for a new day in the church on a plateau.

3
The Ex-Neighborhood Church

Scattered across urban America are the meeting places of hundreds of congregations which can best be described as "ex-neighborhood churches." While many of these, especially in eastern cities, were founded long before the turn of the century, the typical ex-neighborhood church traces its origins back to one of three waves of new church development. The first was the period between 1890 and the beginning of World War I, the second was the 1920s, and the third was the 1948–1963 period.

In the typical situation the congregation was organized to serve the residents of a clearly defined residential section of the city. Many of the older of these congregations drew most of their members from specific language, nationality, or ethnic groups such as German, Italian, American Negro, Welsh, Danish, Swedish, Norwegian, Newfoundland, or Czech. More recently, the new congregations that subsequently became ex-neighborhood churches were organized to serve all of the residents of a specifically defined geographical area or "field." Regardless of the date of the founding of the congregation, however, most of these congregations located their meeting place in what was at the time a comparatively homogeneous neighborhood. Frequently these were relatively new neighborhoods for upper-middle and upper class residents and were located on the outer edge of the large central cities.

As the years passed many of the original members of the congregation died or moved out of the immediate area around the meeting place. The children grew up and married, but many of them continued to maintain their membership in the congregation and their spouses accounted for a large share of the "outsiders" among the new adult members. A decreasing proportion of the members lived within walking distance of the building and a rapidly decreasing proportion of the residents identified with what earlier often had been *the* neighborhood church. A larger proportion of the leaders than of the entire active membership lived several miles away. The median age of the congregation rose several months each year; each year the number of funerals exceeded the number of weddings or the number of baptisms; the dollar receipts began to level off. Two or three or four adult Sunday school classes remained strong, but other adult classes, especially those for persons under forty-five years of age, dissolved while the children's and youth's divisions of the Sunday school classes began to decline rapidly. A major addition to or remodeling of the church school facilities occurred between 1955 and 1965—perhaps in response to a need, perhaps in response to a dream—frequently in the hope that a new building would attract new people. As the years passed, more and more members began to ask more questions about the future.

Factors in the Change Process

An examination of the life and ministry of scores of these ex-neighborhood churches reveals several factors that have contributed significantly to the changes encountered by the ex-neighborhood church. While not all these have been influential in the life and ministry of every one of these congregations, none are unusual.

The most obvious is the decentralization of the urban population which began right after World War I and accelerated in the 1950s, contributing to the establishment of hundreds of what today can be described as ex-neighborhood churches as well as to the change in type of already existing parishes.

This decentralization trend was sparked by the commuter train, the paved street, the private automobile, the rise in the level of income of the typical urban household, the widespread dislike of "city life" and urban life-styles by a majority of Americans, the growing popularity of the single family home, and the incorporation of suburban communities.

This decentralization trend was interrupted for approximately fifteen years by the Great Depression and World War II, but continued at an accelerating pace for the next three decades.

A second factor for change has been the normal aging of the original families in the congregation and the vocational and geographical migration of many of their children. Today it is less common than ever before for the son to follow in his father's vocational footsteps or for the grown children to live in the same municipality as their parents. The obvious consequence is that the natural "replacement population" for the neighborhood church is diminishing. While there is a widespread tendency by the adults to view the teenagers and children as the future members of their congregation, this hope is seldom reflected in reality. If the names of the persons who were in the confirmation class in 1954, 1955, and 1956 are reviewed, it is an unusual church *of this type* that in 1975 reported as many as one-sixth among the current active members. Typically only 15 percent of the high school class of a decade ago are among today's active members. The number of charter members also has decreased rapidly during the past two decades and today is as likely to account for less than 1 percent of the total membership as it is to be as high as 5 percent.

A third factor for change often can be identified with the turnover in pastors. Many ex-neighborhood churches have been served for two or three or four decades by one pastor—and in a few cases by a pastor followed by his son. When this minister, who may or may not have been the founding pastor, retires, dies, or moves to another church, there are two or three major consequences. Most visible is the number of families who had found it a growing inconvenience "to drive back in so far" two or three or four times a week, but had continued to do so out of loyalty to the congregation, affection for the pastor, and fulfillment of their own needs. The change in ministers often makes it easy for some of these people to decide this is a good time to transfer their membership to a church nearer their home. Another common consequence is that if the departing minister had served for two decades or longer, in the vast majority of cases his successor turns out to be an interim minister.[1] The change in ministers usually is accompanied by a change in the programmatic emphasis of the church, by a significant shift in leadership, and by the discontent of many members who reveal the natural, human reluctance to see changes replace tradition.

A fourth factor in the change process has been working to reinforce the stability of the ex-neighborhood church and to help it perpetuate many of the old forms, traditions, roles, and emphases. This is the completion of the freeway network which in many cities has made it very easy for the member living five or ten or fifteen or twenty miles away to drive in for worship, church school, meetings, and special programs. It is probably safe to say that scores of today's ex-neighborhood congregations would have disappeared by now had it not been for the actions of the persons responsible for highway construction. While highway construction has been identified as the cause of the death of many such congregations, it probably has "saved" more than it has eliminated.

[1] For an elaboration of this point, see Lyle E. Schaller, *The Pastor and the People* (Nashville: Abingdon Press, 1973), pp. 56-64.

THE EX-NEIGHBORHOOD CHURCH

Perhaps the strongest and most influential factor in this gradual process of the change of the nature and role of what was founded as a congregation to serve a geographically defined neighborhood has been the attachment to place. Human beings have a very strong attachment to familiar places. This strong attachment to place is expressed in many ways ranging from the "turf" claimed by youth gangs to church members who always sit in the same pew, if possible, to homecomings of many descriptions, to "going back home" to be married or buried.

Unquestionably the most influential single variable in the process of change faced by the typical ex-neighborhood church is how the nonresident members view the neighborhood around the meeting place. As long as the members living two or three or ten or twelve miles away view the neighborhood as reasonably safe and moderately attractive, it is relatively easy to continue as a strong drive-in congregation. When these members begin to see the neighborhood as unattractive or unsafe, rapid changes usually are imminent.

Another factor in the change process has been the establishment of new congregations by the parent denomination three, four, or five miles further out from the heart of the central city. While these new congregations have siphoned off relatively few members from the ex-neighborhood church, they have offered competition for the loyalty of newcomers to that part of the metropolis. These new congregations also offer a convenient scapegoat for those who prefer criticism to analysis.

Perhaps the most subtle factor in this process of change is in the definition of community (see chapter one). When this congregation which is not an ex-neighborhood church was first formed, there was a strong sense of "community" among the residents of this area. As the years and sometimes the decades passed, the neighborhood changed from one of a comparatively homogeneous population to an increasingly heterogeneous population. Concurrent with this was a decrease in the sense of community. It became increasingly easier to walk down a residential street without seeing a familiar face or experiencing an exchange of friendly greetings.

For the members of the ex-neighborhood church, the worshiping congregation which once had been both a reflection of and a part of the community became "the community." What had once been two "communities" (church and neighborhood) with a very high degree of overlap between the two, became two separate communities with very few people members of both communities. While the meeting place for the congregation also might be the meeting place for various community programs, groups, and organizations, very few of the people in attendance at a community meeting also would be present for a church meeting and vice versa.

Finally, in any examination of the process of change in the ex-neighborhood church it is difficult to overstate the sheer toughness of the long established congregation. While a projection of statistical curves in 1960 may have pointed to extinction by 1975, the prophets often turned out to be in error because they underestimated the tenacity and the loyalty of the present members of the ex-neighborhood church.

Forks in the Road

As the years and decades go by, the congregation that was organized to serve a specific residential community often becomes an ex-neighborhood church. When this happens, and it is not always inevitable, the members face several choices. One fork in the road is to continue to try to minister to the same kind of people for as long as possible. This usually leads, sooner or later, to relocation, merger, or dissolution.

A second fork leads to a continuation of the emphasis on a ministry to nearby residents which will be encouraged, supported, and perhaps shared by the nonresident members. This often turns into what some outsiders—and apparently many neighborhood residents—view as a colonial outpost which eventually requires outside (denominational) financial support from colonial headquarters.

A third fork involves a more direct and persistent concern with the institutional survival of a ministry under the original name and flag. This has produced a tremendous variety of responses including (1) sale of the property and relocation of the congregation's meeting place, (2) retention of the original meeting place, with what for all practical purposes is disbandment of the congregation followed by creation of what is in fact a new congregation drawn from nearby residents, (3) dissolution of the congregation with retention of the church property as a place for a denominationally supported ministry without the presence of a worshiping congregation, (4) a minimum level of denominational subsidy to enable the dwindling congregation to operate for a few more years, and (5) reducing costs by use of a part-time pastor.

A fourth fork in this road includes an *intentional* effort to shift to a nongeographical base in defining the characteristics of the membership, plus a continued effort to minister to the needs of nearby residents whether they are members or nonmembers, *plus* one or two or three carefully defined specialized ministries to specifically defined segments of the metropolitan population.

A fifth, and heavily traveled fork in this road is taken by the congregation that decides to perpetuate yesterday as long as possible, "and we'll deal with the crisis when we reach it."

A sixth fork is chosen by a relatively small number of ex-neighborhood congregations. This fork requires a major shift in focus from either a neighborhood orientation or yesterday's patterns to a new definition or purpose, role, and program. The alternatives are many and are limited only by local conditions and vision. The emphasis, however, is always heavy on intentionality and on a response to people's needs rather than on preservation of an institution, retention of a meeting place, or other means to an end which along some of the other roads are converted into ends in themselves.

An excellent example of a congregation taking this sixth fork in the road is an Episcopal parish just north of the District of Columbia. Here was a parish which once had a close identity with the community and, as the community began to become more heterogeneous and the membership of the parish more scattered, began to follow the classic pattern of becoming *the* community for members. This pattern of disengagement from the community, which tends to launch a self-defeating cycle of events, has been reversed. Today this parish is *both* a community and a part of the larger community. This parish is not simply a "community church," however. It is clearly an Episcopal parish which sees itself as a teaching parish in several respects and which displays a high degree of intentionality about who it is, what it is doing, and where it is going.

A seventh fork is chosen by what is perhaps the smallest number of ex-neighborhood churches. This is a deliberate return to the role of being the church in the community for the residents of that community.

An example of this is a United Presbyterian Church in the District of Columbia. In early 1967 it appeared to some outside observers that the decade-long decline in membership would continue at the rate of perhaps 200 members a year and the church would close by the end of 1972. By the end of 1974 the congregation included nearly 800 members, 30 percent of them black, and had been averaging 60 new members per year for seven years.

Characteristics

What are the characteristics of the ex-neighborhood church? Are there any signs which help identify this type of congregation? How can one identify in advance the drift of the neighborhood-oriented congregation into this category?

Perhaps the best way to respond to these questions is to list several of the characteristics which repeatedly are found in this type of congregation, although it should be noted that only rarely does any one congregation display every one of these characteristics.

The most obvious characteristic is that many of the present members once lived in the neighborhood in which the meeting place is located, but now reside two, three, five, ten, twenty, or thirty miles distant.

One of the characteristics most often mentioned by members of the ex-neighborhood church can be summarized in these words: "We used to have every room filled for Sunday school; today we have several empty rooms and in some classes there are only one or two children. Yet there seem to be more children in the neighborhood than ever. I can't understand why they're not in our Sunday school."

The visitor to the ex-neighborhood church sees a worshiping congregation on Sunday morning largely composed of persons who have passed their fiftieth birthday. The women outnumber the men by a seven to three ratio, and the widows are more numerous than the persons in their late twenties or early thirties. As the visitor talks with members, he finds many who have been a part of this congregation for two or three or four decades or who are the grown children of longtime members. He encounters very few adults who have joined during the past three years unrelated to one of the longtime families.

The typical ex-neighborhood church added a church school wing and fellowship hall in the late

1950s or early 1960s—apparently in the hope that the building would draw the people or, in some cases, to house the program of the early and middle 1950s.

Today one hears several people saying, "It's a shame for all these rooms to be empty all week. The least we can do is open the building to the community and make sure the building is used every day of the week." Several members are quietly opposed to this because they "know what those people will do to our building."

Each year the nominating committee in the ex-neighborhood church finds it increasingly difficult to fill all of the slots in the table of organization. Earlier the nominating committee could "pick and choose." Now, by including many women and several young people on the governing board, the nominating committee is able to "present a full slate" although they recognize that several of those who have been nominated will not actually be active officers.

When the worship attendance which usually averages somewhere between 45 and 160 in the ex-neighborhood church is mentioned, this provokes the dismal comment, "I can remember when we used to have to put chairs in the aisles nearly every Sunday" or "I can remember when, if we had less than 300 we considered that a very disappointing crowd." If it is mentioned that the present attendance of 90 is larger than that of more than one-half of the churches in American Protestantism, this comment is brushed off as irrelevant. What matters is the comparison with "how it used to be."

The largest and strongest adult group in the ex-neighborhood church today usually is what began years ago as a group of married couples in their thirties. Today the youngest members of this group are in their late forties or early fifties. In an earlier day this group opposed the formation of a class of young married couples in their late twenties and early thirties on the grounds that, "These people are welcome to join our group. The bigger the better! If you start this new class, it will draw off people we need to replace the members of our group who move away." Despite this opposition a group for younger couples was started, but it slowly died out a few years after reaching a peak of a dozen or so couples. Subsequent efforts to start Sunday school classes or study groups for young couples in their late twenties and early thirties have been consistently unsuccessful. .

One of the characteristics of the ex-neighborhood church is the relatively high level of giving. Typically the receipts from the members average $300 to $400 times the average attendance at Sunday morning worship. An increasing proportion of the receipts from the members comes to the church by mail rather than by the offering plate. (This relatively high level of giving, despite the fact that many members are living on retirement incomes, reflects the fact that the level of giving in most congregations is strongly influenced by the degree of loyalty to that congregation and by the number of years the individual has been a member.)

Perhaps the closest universal characteristic of the ex-neighborhood church is expressed in the frequently articulated wish, "We have to attract more youth and young couples with small children. After all, that's where the future of the church is!"

While far from universal, one of the ties that holds many ex-neighborhood churches together is the mortgage. Keeping up the payments on the mortgage from the last building program or remodeling effort provides direction, motivation, and satisfaction—and sometimes a convenient excuse for what is not done in program, ministry, outreach, or salary increases for staff members.

Members of the ex-neighborhood church observe the centuries-old tradition of seeking a scapegoat for the current dilemma. The two chosen most frequently are either (1) the movement into the neighborhood of a racial, ethnic, national, or religious group different from the membership of this congregation and/or (2) the decision by the denomination during the 1950s and 1960s to establish new congregations in the newer suburban neighborhoods farther out from the central city.

One of the most unproductive forms of unintentional scapegoating often occurs in the small ex-neighborhood church which was forced by economic pressures to turn to a part-time pastor for ministerial leadership. Now, several years later, with the assistance of a denominational grant or by use of the capital funds they have been able to call a vigorous young seminary graduate. The dream is that this youthful minister and his attractive young wife will attract other young married couples which "we need so badly if this church is to continue. You can't build a church on a bunch of old people like us. You need young people!" Two years later the continued numerical decline in the size of the congregation is blamed on this young minister, his youth, and his other limitations.

While identifying itself as a "very friendly" congregation, the ex-neighborhood church actually has very few "points of entry" for new members. The visitor in the 25-50 age range finds very few, if any, groups composed of people under fifty years of age. The two or three or four groups of older persons share a common past and heritage and make many references to the past. This causes the newcomer, who is completely unfamiliar with that heritage, to feel out of place and out of touch with the common agenda of the group. The one group that often is most open to the newcomer is the choir, and a remarkably high proportion of new adult members come into the ex-neighborhood church via the choir. (See chapter one for comments on the impact on newcomers of the "heritage-oriented" members.)

The two categories of member households which

almost invariably dominate the membership picture in the ex-neighborhood church are (1) the one-generation household, typically a husband and wife with no children living at home, but also including the two sisters living together and (2) the one-person household. In third place in numbers are the two-generation households which include parents with children at home. The one outstanding exception to this generalization is the ex-neighborhood church which in recent years has attracted a large number of young married couples with children. These exceptions usually include one or more of the following: (1) an exceptionally attractive and meaningful worship service on Sunday morning, (2) a distinctive *ministry* (not a service program!) to young couples with small children such as a church-sponsored and *church-related* nursery school and related programming, (3) a very strong emphasis on the group life of the congregation, (4) unusual opportunities for adults in the 25-50 age range to be involved in meaningful ministry through the church, or (5) a vigorous, intentional, and highly visible effort by the pastor and other congregational leaders to recreate the high degree of overlap which once existed between the congregation as a community and the neighborhood as a community.

Another characteristic common to most ex-neighborhood churches is that year after year the number of transfers of members out to other congregations exceeds the number of transfers in from other congregations. Not infrequently this ratio is three, four, five, or six to one.

Closely related are the comparatively high median age and the relatively high death rate in the ex-neighborhood congregation. The median age of this type of congregation almost always is above fifty years, often is above sixty, and usually is increasing by a few months every year. Again, the outstanding exception is the ex-neighborhood church which, with obvious intentionality, has stopped drifting into the future and has defined a new role for itself. In these congregations the median age usually is dropping by a few months every year. The death rate in most of the mainline Protestant denominations is approximately 1.2 per 100 confirmed members. In the ex-neighborhood church it tends to be in the range of 2.0 to 3.6 deaths per hundred members each year.

During the past decade inflation has been a continuing fact of life in the American economy. This, plus a general rise in income has meant that the median family income in 1973 was approximately double the median family income of 1961. The dollar receipts of the ex-neighborhood church may be a little higher in 1973 than back in 1961, but during the past few years the receipts from the contributions of members usually has been decreasing at a rate of 3 to 5 percent per year. Add this to an inflationary rate, averaging close to 5 percent each year, and this means a decrease in the real buying power of members' contributions of 8 to 10 percent per year.

If looked at from another perspective, the ex-neighborhood church usually includes many members who are committed to that congregation by shared roots and the heritage of the past, and relatively few who share a commitment to that congregation based on contemporary goals and on what that congregation is doing in ministry and service today. (For an elaboration of this point see chapter one.)

While far from universal, a very common characteristic of the ex-neighborhood church is the relatively youthful age of the present pastor. There are at least three aspects of this which deserve mention here. First, today's youthful pastor frequently is relating to a group of leaders who back in their formative years in the congregation were relating to a minister who was ten or twenty or thirty years older than they were at that time. Today they are two or three decades older than the present minister. Second, major differences in the year of birth frequently do make a difference (see chapter one). Third, frequently today's relatively youthful minister thought he was called to help relate this church to the people now living in the neighborhood around the meeting place. While this desire may have been articulated in the discussions which led to the call, many of the long-time members also hoped that he would be able to turn the calendar back twenty years and would possess all of the skills, attributes, and gifts which they remember as characteristics of their favorite minister from the cherished past. Unless these differences in expectations are resolved, they often produce a variety of tensions, disagreements, and conflicts in the ex-neighborhood church.

If these are also the characteristics of your congregation, what can you do? How do you begin to outline the next chapter in this story of your church?

Next Steps?

Where are the "handles" for the leaders in the ex-neighborhood church as they plan for today and tomorrow? For some congregations it may be appropriate to turn back to chapter two and review the "Lessons From Experience." For others it may be helpful to ask, "Are we as a congregation becoming a community which is increasingly disengaged from the community in which our meeting place is located?" If the answer is in the affirmative, the Episcopal parish mentioned earlier may serve as a model. For a third ex-neighborhood church the beginning points for next steps may be found among the suggestions in chapter one regarding community, commitment, and generational differences.

Or it may be more helpful to look at what happened in three specific situations.

The first is the Presbyterian church in Washington, D.C. which was mentioned earlier. This congregation made a remarkable change in direction from moving toward becoming an ex-neighborhood church and developed a new role as a community oriented congregation. In doing this they learned several lessons which can be instructive to leaders in other congregations.

Among the "lessons" demonstrated by this experience are (1) the absolute necessity that the church members accept 100 percent of the responsibility to "prove" to new neighborhood residents they are wanted, (2) the value of an intensive, extensive, redundant, and persistent visitation program, (3) the value of listening, (4) the tremendous values of symbolic events which made people go home feeling glad they are members of *this* congregation, (5) the importance of the self-esteem of a congregation in developing expectations about the future, (6) the fundamental importance of the members believing that what they are doing reflects the Lord's will, (7) broad ownership of both goals and victories, (8) the highly visible celebration of victories, (9) intentionality, and (10) the values of good pastoral leadership.

In another, somewhat smaller midwestern city, a larger ex-neighborhood congregation laid out this three-point program in planning for the future.

1. Change the agenda.

The current "agenda" or series of questions most often discussed by members included (a) a thrice rejected and now obsolete plan for relocation to the suburbs, (b) an irrelevant proposal to remodel the old structure—which would have been a complete diversion from the central question, and (c) scapegoating for the ineffectiveness of the ministry to children and youth—the primary reason for the decrease in the size of the Sunday school and the high school youth group was that nearly all of the members stopped having children fifteen years ago. The old agenda was a loser. It included too many times representing drift, nostalgia, indecision, bickering over means to an end, scapegoating, lack of self-understanding, low self-esteem, and a desire to relive the past.

2. Change the focus!

The focus for ministry had been almost exclusively on the members. The new focus was on calling on residents of the hundreds of two-story apartment buildings which had been constructed in this older neighborhood following an urban renewal clearance program. The members called, elicited the concerns of the residents, listened, and cared. Within a year the primary focus of the congregation had turned from inward to outward. A total of 159 different members completed a combined total of 3,640 personal visits on individuals, couples, and families living within a half mile of the meeting place of the congregation. At many households six to ten calls were made during that year.

3. Change the program!

For years the program of this dwindling congregation had been built around a six point outline consisting of (1) Sunday worship, (2) Sunday school, (3) maintenance of the meeting place, (4) meeting the budget, (5) keeping a resident minister, (6) the meetings of the women's organization. Most of the elements of this program called for a relatively passive role for most of the members most of the time. There was a strong emphasis on "keeping the doors open."

The revised program included all of the above components plus at least one major "event" every month. These included a Lay Witness Mission, an all-church picnic, the development of a drama club which offered a serious religious play twice a year, a Discovering Christ weekend, a Tenebrae service on Maundy Thursday, a multi-media special worship event one Sunday morning, a communion breakfast, a six-week vacation Bible school for adults one summer, a very moving Christmas Eve service, a weekend chartered bus trip to visit a national missions project which included more than half the members, a series of study groups in Transactional analysis, a youth encounter weekend, development of a series of Bible study classes using the Bethel Series, a "clean the church" weekend, and a special "fill the church Sunday" twice a year in which every member was expected to invite a friend to worship.

The content of these events is not especially significant here. What is important is the style of parish life. In less than six months the stifling boredom had been replaced with an air of excitement, and the expectation of a passive role for members had been replaced by the expectation of an active role. Apathy was replaced by enthusiasm. Instead of simply talking about and listening to lectures on Christianity, the program was enriched by opening a variety of opportunities for people to enjoy the experience of being a sharing Christian.

4

The Ex-Rural Church

Located about forty-five minutes driving time north of Charlotte, North Carolina in what appears to be a sparsely populated rural area is a modest brick building resembling the meeting place for a rural congregation. An hour's investigation, however, reveals that off the state highway and around the lake are several hundred homes, most of them less than three years old. A dozen years ago a 120-year-old, ninety-member rural congregation replaced its old frame chapel with this new brick building. Today 70 percent of 300 members come from homes where at least one parent commutes to Charlotte to work five days a week.

About forty minutes west of Fort Wayne, Indiana there is a large Gothic-style stone church on the road to a cluster of small lakes. This fifteen-year-old structure was built by two tiny rural congregations that merged in 1953 and moved to a new site by the state highway. It is located two miles south of the center of the crossroads community, which was a sleepy small town for nearly a century. And it still is except for the summer months when the area population jumps from seven hundred in the winter to four thousand on a Wednesday in July to twenty thousand on an August weekend. This is the summer home for thousands of "snowbirds," who flock to Florida and Arizona in the fall and go home to indiana in the spring, as well as for many weekend vacationers.

About thirty minutes west of Knoxville, Tennessee a congregation that was established in 1841 and had exactly 100 members when it celebrated its centennial, recently built a four-hundred-seat sanctuary to complete its $380,000 new building on a five-acre site.

These three congregations have much in common with thousands of other ex-rural churches.

They all are being affected by the current wave of decentralization. People are moving out of the large central cities and older suburbs to enjoy the benefits of country living and a city paycheck. All across the country, people are taking advantage of the new highway network to move twenty or thirty or forty or even fifty or sixty miles from the heart of the old central business district. Those formerly rural communities located on or near a lake are experiencing a major population explosion. As the population moves out, an increasing number of factories and businesses are joining this exodus from the old urban center. As the jobs move out to what appears to be a rural setting, this accelerates the movement of people to rural areas.

The post-1970s trend is a sharp reversal from that of the previous three decades. During the 1950s the net migration from nonmetropolitan areas to metropolitan centers totalled 5.5 million. During the 1960s this figure dropped to a net of 2.2 million people.

Sometime about 1968 or 1969 this migration stream began to flow the other way. Between early 1970 and mid-1974 at least a million more people moved from metropolitan counties to nonmetropolitan counties than migrated in the other direction.

This is *not* a back-to-the-farm movement. The farm population has continued to decline—from 31.4 million in 1920 to 23 million in 1950 to 15.6 million in 1960 to 9.7 million in 1970 to 8.8 million in 1974. By contrast, the nonfarm population has climbed from 20.2 million in 1920 to 31.2 million in 1950 to 44.2 million in 1970 to 46.0 million in 1974. In 1920 for every three persons living on farms there were two rural nonfarm residents. Fifty-four years later for every three persons living on a farm there were sixteen rural nonfarm residents!

In recent years this out-migration has been accelerated by civil disorders, the rapid increase in crime and vandalism, and the fear of busing. (A majority of the children in many of these large consolidated schools in the formerly rural areas travel to school by bus, but this is an acceptable form of busing to the people moving out here.) Frequently the combination of these factors has sparked a population boom in the second or third county out beyond the county in which the central city is located.

A second common characteristic of many of the churches in these ex-rural communities is that for decades they were stable congregations, typically with fewer than 100 members. Most of the leaders had been reared in that church.

In some, the attitude of the old-timers toward the newcomers is expressed in such terms as, "The door is open; if they are really Christians and want to come to church on Sunday, all they have to do is walk in." or "The best members usually turn out to be those who come on their own; the people you go out and drag in usually turn out to be simply names on the roll." or "Most of these folks won't stay long, so why should we make any fuss over them?"

In others, a determined effort was made to reach out to contact and accept the new members and to make the changes that resulted from this effort. When this was done, one of the most frequent results was the decision to buy additional land or move to a larger site and build larger facilities.

The congregation that spends several years planning and implementing a building program often develops a degree of skill, a sense of adequacy, and a feeling of fulfillment in acquiring and improving a site, in planning and constructing a new building, and in paying the financial obligations incurred in this lengthy process.

A normal outgrowth of such planning is an overemphasis on maintaining and expanding the building. At this, leaders feel competent and self-confident. This in turn feeds an emphasis on survival and on tangible goals rather than on discovering a new role and a new identity.

It may be wiser to see this first step as phase one. The future then becomes a new era. Its emphasis will be on ministry and program development or use of the new facilities rather than on maintenance of the building. In this new era the emphasis is on the intangible and less visible goals of ministry and servanthood. This is much easier to suggest, however, than it is to accomplish!

It means the leaders have to develop and operate from a new frame of reference, to develop a new variety of skills and capabilities, and to emphasize a new set of priorities in the allocation of time, money, and energy. It is much easier and much more comfortable to remain back in that phase which emphasizes planning, constructing, and caring for a meeting place and requires skills many leaders already possess. It is more difficult to talk about developing the sense of urgency and the skills implied in such terms as mission, evangelism, worship, Bible study, and social action.

Some of these new buildings have Sunday school facilities that reflect the "grandmother syndrome." While most grandmothers no longer have small children of their own, grandmothers buy many of the prettiest dresses for little girls and a large proportion of the most expensive toys for little boys that are sold today. Likewise some of these churches have large, very attractive, and remarkably well-furnished children's Sunday school rooms—but no children.

Another set of common characteristics of the ex-rural church can be grouped under the term "depression ethic." Many of the long-time members and influential leaders of the ex-rural church were born before 1928 and have vivid firsthand memories of the Great Depression. This encourages support for building only what can be paid for from cash on hand or at the most with a four or five year mortgage; a reluctance to pay a salary to anyone other than the minister, thus relying exclusively on volunteers for janitorial, clerical, and program obligations; a confirmation of the pattern of each organization having its own treasurer and treasury, including many of the adult Sunday school classes; and a reluctance to endorse diversity in program and ministry. In every survival-oriented organization there is a tendency to urge conformity as a means of reinforcing unity. Only when the members of an organization believe it has moved beyond the survival orientation is it possible to endorse the concept that unity and diversity are compatible. The ex-rural church tends to be an outstanding example of this generalization.

Another common characteristic of the ex-rural church can be seen in the composition of the membership. If the population of the community is divided into groups such as the "old-timers," the "permanent residents," the "newcomers," the "summer people" or the "lake people," and the "weekend vacationers," the first two groups may represent only 10 percent of the population on Sunday in July and perhaps 40 percent on a Monday in February. But these two groups often account for 80 percent of the people at worship on Sunday morning and 98 percent of those at a board meeting on Tuesday evening in the long-established churches.

From Today to Tomorrow

What's ahead for these ex-rural churches located in what often appears to be at least a semirural if not a rural setting, but in fact is a new expression of urbanism? The answer to that question can be summarized in three words.

Change or decay.

These are threatening words. Many of the longtime

residents of three or four decades and the newer permanent residents who moved to the community six or eight years ago feel threatened by the current changes in the community resulting from a growing number of people moving out from the city. The schools are overcrowded. Taxes are going up. A new sewage disposal system has to be built. The highways are overloaded, and land use controls are being adopted. A diminishing proportion of the people on the streets and in the stores are old acquaintances. More and more people do not exchange greetings when they meet on the street, and familiar landmarks are being razed to make way for new buildings.

When changes in the community are compounded by the threat of additional changes in the church, a typical response is to think in terms of a ceiling on size. "We built our church, let them build theirs." or "It's not good to get too big."

Another typical response of many people in the ex-rural church is to develop an approach to the newcomers, the seasonal couples, and the vacationing families based on a philosophy expressed by the words, "Come to us on our terms." The longterm members are accustomed to a Sunday morning schedule of Sunday school at 9:30 and worship at 10:30. "Why change it for a few months simply to accommodate a handful of strangers who may not even show up?"

"Two services in the morning means more work for our minister and a divided congregation."

"Why should we go to the bother of having special outdoor services in the summer? It seems to me that anyone who really wants to worship the Lord can come over here at 10:30."

Lessons From Experience

How do these ex-rural congregations respond creatively to the challenge of change? Many have been able to adapt to a new role in a new era. What have they learned which might be shared with others?

First and most important, the ex-rural congregations that have been most effective with newcomers have been those that began their approach by seeking to respond to the needs of people rather than to expect the newcomers to come to them.

A second common characteristic of those ex-rural congregations that have experienced an effective transition and have been able to reach the newcomers is the willingness to make changes to accommodate the new people. This is in sharp contrast to those congregations which have said in effect, "Come to us on our terms, or don't come." When given those choices, most newcomers have selected the second.

The changes may be in schedule, in building facilities, and in the length of the "probationary period" a new member must serve before being considered eligible to hold a church office, but the critical factor is the willingness of the old members to make changes to accommodate people.

A third characteristic of those ex-rural congregations that have had a successful building program is that they saw the building as a means for ministry rather than as an end in itself. An interesting yardstick in measuring this is to ask the question, "How long after the building was completed did it become available for community meetings and other nonchurch affairs?" In the congregations that stand out as models for adapting to change, this decision came within two years after completion of the structure. In others, the trustees were subjected to such strong criticism because of scuff marks on the floor or wall or scratches on the new woodwork that it took five to ten years before the focus shifted from the care to the use of the building.

Closely related is the ability of the congregation to mobilize the resources necessary for a contemporary ministry. Frequently the tradition of a very limited scope of church program combined with pressure to build a building or retire a debt (or to rest from those exertions) means the program may be inadequate when compared to the size of either the building or the membership.

A fifth common characteristic of the ex-rural church that has made a successful transition is that people know one another by name. This may appear to be a trivial matter, but in fact it often is of crucial importance. A group of people can be a worshiping congregation and still not know each other. But a caring fellowship emerges only where people can address one another by name. Not infrequently the planning and construction of the new building also was the process by which the old-timers and the newcomers became acquainted. Church directories with pictures of members help. Several churches feature a family of the week on the bulletin board every week, and this is a useful technique. In at least a couple of churches in vacation areas every member wears a name tag every Sunday all summer long and visitors are encouraged to identify themselves with name cards. Another church has a formal training program to help every greeter and usher develop the skill of remembering names. In many congregations social get-togethers every two or three weeks during the summer enable people to become better acquainted.

A related lesson that has been reinforced repeatedly by the experiences of many ex-rural churches is the importance of good internal communication. The smaller congregation composed largely of persons who had resided in that community for decades could rely on a highly informal communication. As the congregation increased in size and included more people who were not tied into the community grapevine at several points, one of two patterns usually emerged. In some cases failures in communication within the congregation produced unnecessary and avoidable misunderstandings, hurt feelings, tensions, and conflicts that inhibited the work, outreach, and ministry of the church. In other congregations there was an intentional effort to develop a systematic and redundant communication system that includes the telephone, postcards, personal visits, newsletters, posters, personal mailings, the local newspaper, the church bulletin, color slides, banners, the Sunday school. A dozen other channels of internal communication increased as the congregation grew in size and complexity.

Finally, the effective ex-rural church is able to discard the notion that it is raising its own leaders of the future. It sees the youth of today as future leaders, but recognizes the fact that most of them will be members of other congregations in 1990. The acceptance of this radical change from the past is a major factor in helping the people recognize and accept new leaders from among the newcomers to the community, some of whom are viewed by everyone including themselves as only temporary.

These lessons from experience, many of which are applicable to most churches facing rapid community change, are especially significant for the ex-rural church moving into a new era in its long history.

5

The Teenage Church

The origins of the Pleasant Valley Church can be traced back to a meeting of eight people in the living room of Stanley and Dorothy Cole in October, 1961. All eight agreed on the need for a new congregation to serve this rapidly growing suburban community. Every one of those present drove at least four miles each way to church and the Coles lived eleven miles from their home church which was located on the other side of the central business district.

With the encouragement and financial assistance of the denomination, a pastor was found who wanted to help launch a new congregation. He arrived in February, 1962, and the first worship service was held on the first Sunday in Lent with fifty-three people representing seventeen families in attendance. This new congregation met in a school until October, 1963, when the first unit of their permanent new meeting place was completed. This $110,000 structure was crowded from the very first day and plans were made for the second unit of what was expected to be a three-unit building. This second unit was designed to serve as combination worship facility-fellowship hall for six to eight years. By that time, according to the projections, the congregation should include 700 to 900 confirmed members and be both ready and financially able to begin construction of a six-hundred-seat sanctuary. The projections for the future indicated this new mission would level off in size with 1400 to 1600 confirmed members in the early 1980s. This second unit was completed in 1965 at a cost of $160,000. Plans for the completion of the $450,000 third unit have been shelved, perhaps only temporarily, but certainly for at least another decade.

Today the Pleasant Valley Church lists 277 confirmed members on the roll, down from a peak of 312 four years ago. The worship attendance averages 115, down from the peak of 157, while the Sunday school averages between 90 and 100 compared to the average attendance of 150 in 1968. Last year the dollar receipts totaled $29,000, which meant that was the third year in a row that only interest payments were made on the three mortgages—one of $8,000 on the parsonage, a second of $12,000 left from the first building program, and the third of $77,000 from the last building program. The first two are with the denomination, but the third is with a local savings and loan association and a notice has been received that principle and interest payments must be made in full this year or the mortgage must be refinanced at much higher interest rates.

The present pastor, George Wilson, came on the scene in 1974 as the fourth in the succession of ministers. The first one stayed six years, the second four years, and the third left after two years. George is a forty-six-year-old man with twenty years of effective service in the ministry behind him. He was persuaded by the denominational executive in the regional judicatory that his skills and leadership were badly needed at Pleasant Valley. The previous pastor had been unhappy where he was previously and apparently came to Pleasant Valley, not in response to a sense of a "call" to Pleasant Valley, but rather to escape where he was. Twenty-one months after his arrival he announced to a startled congregation that he and his wife were seeking a divorce and that he was leaving the ministry. Five days later the parsonage was empty.

George Wilson arrived on the scene to find a congregation with low morale, some sense of guilt that perhaps they had contributed to the breakup of the parsonage family, a financial crisis even more serious than perceived by the leaders, a membership roll carrying nearly 280 names of which one-third represented persons completely inactive or no longer residents, an inadequate budget depending on fifteen families for 60 percent of the congregational income, and a newly paved parking lot, a "gift" from twelve other churches in the denomination in that metropolitan area.

George also found, for the first time in his life, that he was older than nearly every person in his congregation. He also very quickly discovered that his optimism was not as contagious as the pessimism of many of the members! He found at Pleasant Valley a church with a program which was inadequate in both quantity and diversity, a choir of seven faithful but untrained voices, a remarkable degree of discontinuity in the leadership of the church school, tired board leadership, few points of social contact among the members, no money in the budget for program (the Sunday school materials were purchased out of the Sunday school treasury), a poorly designed structure which had far more room than necessary for worship—but not one decent room for group or committee meetings other than the classrooms, a widespread feeling that if permanent pews could be installed to replace the chairs this would give a more worshipful appearance to the fellowship hall and thus boost attendance, and a widely shared dream that the "new minister" was an experienced miracle worker.

Before moving to a discussion of what happened next, it may be helpful to look at the general characteristics of the teenage church.

Characteristics of the Teenage Church

Many new congregations are established every decade in the United States. Some reach "maturity" during the first decade of their life and go on as autonomous, self-directing organizations. Others grow more slowly and continue to be dependent upon outside assistance in various forms well into the second decade of their existence. These "teenage churches" are, by definition, somewhere between twelve and twenty years old. They bear the common characteristic that they have not yet achieved the institutional strength that was anticipated when they were launched to be completely self-sufficient and self-directing with a full-time minister.

In addition to this highly visible common characteristic, however, many of these teenage churches share several other common traits. While not every trait listed here is common to every church in this category, most of these congregations display several of these characteristics. Pleasant Valley Church is representative of this group or type of church.

1. Frequently what is now a teenage church originally began to function as one large group of persons with common interests, shared goals, and affirmative attitudes. Everyone knew everyone else in the group. As time passed, new persons were received into membership in the congregation (but frequently not into the original group!), and the size of the congregation increased until it was too large to function effectively as one group. During this gradual transition, however, few additional new groups were created. (One of the most common differences between the fifteen-year-old 500-member congregation and the fifteen-year-old 200-member congregation is in the attention given ten or twelve years ago to cultivating the group life of the congregation.)

2. Today it appears impossible in the teenage church to match the enthusiasm that was aroused during that first building program several years ago. The present members who were part of that group recall those days of unity and enthusiasm with nostalgia. The present members who joined *after* the com-

pletion of the last building program tend to be either (a) somewhat inactive, (b) concerned with and involved in program, or (c) worried about finances and unable to "recall" the enthusiasm of those "good old days."

3. In meeting with members of teenage congregations it often is easy to distinguish the "old pioneers," the persons who joined before completion of the first building program, from the "homesteaders" who have joined during the past few years.

4. A widely shared need felt among many of the current members is expressed in the phrase, "We simply have to get more members. We're too small to carry the financial load and to do and be what a church should be today."

5. This type of congregation often feels its building facilities are inadequate for contemporary needs, but also feels powerless to do anything about the situation because of (a) current indebtedness and (b) small numbers.

6. The teenage congregation usually (but not always!) has a level of giving well below that of congregations of similar type, size and age, but an above average amount of indebtedness.

7. There frequently is either (a) a feeling of guilt over not being able to pay denominational obligations or (b) a feeling of resentment that the denominational askings are too large for this relatively new congregation.

8. During the past dozen years the role of lay persons in the congregation gradually has moved from active toward the direction of passive.

9. The past emphasis on capital improvements, an interest which often was legitimatized and reinforced by denominational agencies, has tended to place a heavy current emphasis on allocating funds for capital improvements rather than for program. (Most denominational grants and gifts were for capital improvements rather than for program. Today restricted

gifts from members tend to be for capital improvements rather than for program.)

10. There is very little program money in the budget of the typical teenage church.

11. In the typical teenage church the pastor often spends more of his time on clerical and janitorial duties than does the pastor in the long established congregation of a similar size.

12. The tendency in the teenage church is to invite newcomers to the neighborhood to Sunday morning corporate worship rather than to specific events, experiences, programs, and ministries at other hours of the week.

13. The teenage church tends to offer members and nonmembers fewer choices in worship and program than are offered by long established churches of similar size or by larger congregations of the same age.

14. One of the reasons morale appears to be low in the typical teenage church is that there have been few psychic rewards and few satisfactions for the individual members. Likewise there have been relatively few congregational victories. (It often is easier for leaders to name the year when the building was completed than to identify three distinctive contributions in ministry during the past twelve months.)

15. Usually many leaders can recall very clearly the dilemma encountered by the trustees a few years ago. On the one hand, the trustees were pressured to grant permission for the new building to be used for community activities. On the other hand, they also were pressured to preserve this new structure in mint condition.

16. The teenage congregation is highly vulnerable to falling into the trap of "pushing its product" (enlarging the membership roll, getting more people into the Sunday school, or "filling those rooms during the week") rather than in identifying and responding to the needs of people.

17. Many teenage congregations of the 1970s were started in a day and place where it was expected there would be continuing rapid increase in the population in that community. The radical changes that occurred in the housing market during the 1960s and early 1970s often have meant that population growth expectations were not achieved.

18. Many teenage congregations have a meeting place located near several new apartment structures, but relatively few of the residents of these structures are members of the teenage congregation.

19. The teenage congregation usually is built around a core of persons living in two-generation households, with most of them residing in single family homes.

20. While the typical teenage church with 90 to 135 at worship on the average Sunday morning is larger than 60 to 70 percent of all congregations in American Protestantism, many leaders are concerned that the lack of continuing growth may mean the church will close.

21. Frequently the teenage church is served by a full-time minister who is a seminary graduate, sometimes with two or three or four previous pastorates, who occasionally has the feeling that he is underemployed.

22. A careful examination of the facts often reveals that more than one-half of the "church shoppers" who visit the teenage congregation eventually select a different congregation as their new church home.

23. The typical teenage church lacks a distinctive identity in terms of type, community image, or specialization in ministry. It tends to see itself and to be seen by others as a suburban, family-oriented congregation.

What does all of this say to the twelve- to twenty-year-old congregation that believes it is behind schedule in growth and service and that finds a dozen or more of these characteristics fits its situation?

In general, a five-point self-diagnosis may be helpful.

1. How many groups, organizations, committees, and classes (these include all governing boards, administrative committees, church school classes, choirs, study groups, etc.) are there in the church? List each one on a sheet of paper and identify the membership of each by name. How many were formed in response to the traditions, needs, and denominational expectations of the church as an institution? How many were created intentionally in response to the specific needs of identifiable (by name) individuals? (If less than one-half were formed in response to this last question, it may suggest one dimension of the problem.)

Go over this entire list of organizations again. Which are the ones that people look forward to being present when the group meets? Which are the ones where tardiness, absenteeism, or discontinuity in attendance is frequent? Ask not, What is wrong with those people who are tardy or irregular in their attendance? Ask instead, What are the characteristics of the group or organization or meeting that tend to encourage this?

Now go over the list one more time. Check the groups and organizations which clearly are responsive to the needs of the individuals for personal and spiritual growth. Which are not? What proportion of the membership of the congregation are members of groups which are responsive to these needs for personal and spiritual growth?

Now ask the question, What can be done to improve the group health of the entire congregation?

2. List the goals and accomplishments of the congregation for the past twelve months. There should be at least thirty different accomplishments and goals on this list, including those everyone takes for granted.

How many of these are ones in which people are used to achieve the goals of the organization? How many are ones in which the institution is a means toward achieving a sense of fulfillment for people in being what God intended for them?

3. List the six alternatives that are opened up by the existence of this congregation for persons to be *directly* involved or *directly* supportive of ministry to others and mission in the world. How many, by their own choice of these alternatives, *found themselves in a meaningful and enriching involvement?*

4. What were the congregational victories that were celebrated with great visibility and a sense of joy and accomplishment last year?

5. Prepare a list of the fifty adults who joined this congregation most recently. Why did each one pick this congregation? What was the initial major point of contact? (An invitation from a person? A visit from the pastor? A walk-in visitor? Participation in a group or class? With what group or role or organization or class does that person identify today? Is that person an active member today? How many members can that new member call by name today?

This is not intended to serve as a *final* step in efforts by leaders of the teenage congregation to move into a new era of ministry and mission. It is suggested only as part of the beginning of a process.

The first step in this process is to be conscious of self-identity. Is this a congregation that fits the typology or category of a teenage church?

The second step is some form of self-examination, such as the self-diagnosis suggested above. This step should enable and encourage the leaders to ask the questions which constitute the foundation for the third step in this process.

This third step is to formulate in precise operational language an action agenda for the next twelve to eighteen months. The details of this action agenda will vary from one congregation to another, but in each case implementation, or the failure to implement, becomes the decisive vote on the question,

"Should we seek to move out of our present role and into a new role in a new era or should we relax and hope to be a happy teenager, even when we are twenty-five or thirty?"

An example of the application of this process can be seen in what happened at Pleasant Valley shortly after George Wilson came on the scene as the fourth minister of that struggling twelve-year-old congregation.

Next Steps

At Pleasant Valley George Wilson concluded that the most urgent issue on the agenda of this young congregation was a series of "congregational victories." He believed if several short-term goals could be set and achieved this would raise morale and provide a more optimistic base for planning. During George's first eighteen months as pastor these were among the most significant congregational victories.

1. Interest *and principal* payments were made promptly on the mortgage held by the savings and loan association.

2. That first fall an outside stewardship consultant came in (for the second time in the history of Pleasant Valley and the first time in ten years), and with his help the pledges for the coming year were raised to $46,000. (While twelve of the fifteen families giving the most money to the church increased their pledges, the percentage of the total pledged by these fifteen dropped from 60 to 43 percent. In other words, the base of financial support was broadened and this was the major factor in the remarkable increase in giving.)

3. A "Fisherman's Club" of eighteen people was formed. This group was committed to calling on non-churchgoing families and prospective new members. Once a month they met at 6 P.M. for a carry-in meal, Bible study, prayer, and two hours of calling. After they completed their calls, they returned to the host home for that month for an hour of sharing.

4. On the first Sunday in Lent George preached a sermon based on Matthew 25:15-30. Following the sermon he passed out among the members two offering plates filled with five-dollar bills. This was money he had secretly borrowed on a personal note. He asked those who saw themselves as one-talent persons to take a five-dollar bill, for those who saw themselves as two-talent persons to take two five-dollar bills and so on. Before he reached the rear of the nave the plates were empty, and he had to begin passing out a series of IOU slips. Afterward one of the more pessimistic members, who had taken a single five-dollar bill from the plate, said to George, "Preacher, either you have lots of money and lots of faith or else you're a fool. But I do hope you don't lose too much on this deal."

What happened? Here is what George wrote in a personal letter two months later.

"Just a note to report to you about our 'Talents' offering at Pleasant Valley. As you know, I passed out $500 of talent money. Actually I ran out before I got it all the way around, and so I took the names of the people remaining on the back two rows and took money to their homes and let them select the amount as on Sunday. It took $88.50 additional money to satisfy everyone.

"For a week or so everyone was perplexed as to what they were going to do with their talent money, but soon most everyone got an idea and went to work. They did everything from baking to bird houses. It was fascinating to watch the process.

"Last Sunday (April 22) we received our 'Talents' offering and it was a little over $2200. After my $588 was extracted, we had about $1600 net. I think that's a pretty good return on your money (4 for one), don't you? (Another $100 came in later.)"

5. Two summer all-church picnics and a remarkably well-attended all-church dinner at noon on Thanksgiving Day helped strangers become acquain-

tances and acquaintances to move closer to being friends.

6. The average attendance at worship climbed slowly by an average of one a month, but that brought it up closer to 150.

7. A special planning committee was established which developed this strategy statement that later was approved and adopted by the church board.

A Strategy Statement for Pleasant Valley

1. The first 10 percent of each Sunday's offering will be set aside for benevolence.
2. We will develop two new growth groups each year.
3. We will have a ten-day vacation Bible school every summer.
4. The Sunday morning worship service will include a "children's sermonette" every week.
5. In greeting or calling on visitors and prospective members we must be able to issue precise invitations to these people to come to share in specific programs and events.
6. Secure a secretary three mornings a week to enable the pastor to concentrate at least ten hours a week on a specific apartment complex for three months at each complex.
7. Encourage specific designated giving for outreach and program as well as capital improvements.
8. Help the congregation see itself as a congregation of groups as well as one large group of people.
9. Develop at least one six- or eight-week special evening Bible study group a year.
10. Develop means for more members to know one another via social and small group get-togethers.
11. Within eighteen months a second "Fisherman's Club" should be formed.

12. Finish paying off the two smaller mortgages within twenty-four months.
13. Beginning next March we will go to two Sunday morning worship services, with the second a continuation of the present traditional service and the first a more informal and participatory type of service.
14. During the summer months when many people are away over the weekend, a special two-hour midweek church school and worship service will be offered.
15. The Sunday school will offer two twelve-week leadership development courses for adults every year.
16. Conduct an all-member visitation program twice a year to enable the ideas, complaints, suggestions, gripes, feelings, and concerns of every one of the members to be heard.

That is the response developed by one congregation as it identified itself as a teenage church.

6
From Youth to Maturity

During the quarter century following the close of World War II, thousands of new congregations were started all across the continent. Some grew for many years and eventually leveled off with 400 to 700 members. Others found the teenage years to be the crisis period described in the previous chapter. A third group continued to grow and eventually reached the point that the work load was beyond the capability of a single minister. Westminster Church is representative of this third group. The experiences of this congregation, now in its third decade, may offer a useful frame of reference for leaders of other similar congregations as they examine the questions and issues facing them.

Westminster Church was founded as a new mission in 1953. A total of 91 persons signed the charter membership roll when the congregation was formally organized. During the following years, as it moved from its early beginning through the youthful years and into maturity, it encountered a series of hurdles, obstacles, and pitfalls which are common to new congregations. Not every congregation encounters every one of these obstacles, and some pass over several of the hurdles without breaking stride in their growth. They appear not to even be aware of the existence of several of these hurdles.

Group or Congregation?

The first of these hurdles is the organizational shift from the intimate group which formed the nucleus of the new mission. The new congregation usually begins as a collection of individuals and families who form a meaningful large group. As the congregation grows in both numbers and enthusiasm, a new building is constructed and the congregation levels off at a size which is reflected by an average of 70 to 130 at worship on Sunday morning. In the larger metropolitan areas of North America this is too small to be a viable economic and program (ministry) unit for a young congregation with a large debt, a full-time seminary graduate as the pastor, and a sense of being a responsible part of the universal Church. At this point in the life of the new congregation it either completes the transformation from being one large group into becoming a congregation of individuals, families, *and groups of individuals* or it levels off in size. The failure to complete this transformation has been a major factor in creating the problems faced by many teenage congregations.

Westminster Church was fortunate in avoiding this pitfall. Its growth continued without serious interruption to the point that it was obvious to many that this must be viewed as a congregation of groups. This process was facilitated by three important factors. The first was the demand by members for a variety of groups ranging from home Bible study groups to mission task force groups to leadership development groups to growth groups for the young married couples who constituted the core of the membership to making the governing board into a caring group ministering to all of the members. The second factor was a pastor who not only believed in the small group concept, but also had the skill to help in the creation, solidification, and dissolution of groups *and the insight to recognize that what might be a very meaningful small group for some people would hold no attractiveness for others.* He facilitated the development of a remarkably diversified group life at Westminster. The third factor was the denominational polity which

(1) encouraged longer pastorates and (2) encouraged the concept that persons elected to the governing body were first of all ministers and secondly administrative officers. This facilitated the process by which the governing body became a meaningful and supportive group for the leaders *and* a caring fellowship in which every member was expected to call at approximately a score of households four times a year. This calling program by the leaders not only helped the congregation cope with the implications of the growth in size and in the assimilation of new members, it also reduced the normal tendency for some small groups to be viewed by others as cliques.

Thus, as Westminster passed the 100 mark and the 200 mark and then the 300 mark in membership, the members began to change their own perception of the nature of the organization. As happened with so many other new congregations, Westminster began as an excellent example of a healthy small group. Such characteristics of the healthy small group as inclusion, control, affection, openness to newcomers, a meaningful task, and a redemptive character were the characteristics of Westminster in its early years. Unlike many other new congregations, however, Westminster was able to maintain a healthy group life and also grow in size. It cleared this first hurdle with only a few of the members even realizing it was there.

Pioneers and Homesteaders

Closely related is a second hurdle, which while it usually appears several years later, has its origins in the first several months of the life of the new congregation. Being a part of the effort to create a new called-out community of worshiping Christians is an exciting venture. It is truly a pioneering effort. Those early months in a temporary meeting place bind this small group of pioneers into a cohesive fellowship. What appeared at first to be a highly speculative venture with a strong possibility of failure becomes a joint effort of lay persons and pastor who work together. They see their efforts rewarded with a satisfying series of tangible and highly visible goals which are formulated and achieved. These include that first worship service, the arrival of the first permanent pastor, the establishment of the Sunday school, recognition by the denomination as a formally organized congregation, the launching of the first building fund, the ground breaking for that first building, watching and often actively participating in the construction of that first permanent meeting place, the first Sunday in the new building, the frequent reception of new members and the continued growth in size of the congregation, and the first baptism. These are all-important and memorable experiences and events. The entire process resembles the establishment of a new ranch or the founding of a new town out on the western frontier. Truly, these are pioneering days!

Then come the homesteaders.

New families moving into the community begin to attend worship and to bring their children to Sunday school. Some of them are invited to accept leadership responsibilities. But, none of these homesteaders have firsthand recollections of those pioneering days. At a church picnic or at a meeting of the governing body or at a circle meeting it is easy for the pioneers present to turn the conversation back to the hardships and the joys of those early days. The homesteaders present feel left out. Their feelings resemble those of the seven-year-old David, the youngest in a family of six children as he watches his father show the whole family some home movies taken ten years earlier. Repeatedly he asked, "Where am I in those pictures?" After being told that he had not yet been born when these movies were taken, he begins to insist that his Dad show some much newer home movies. The homesteaders are far more polite. They simply say nothing and begin to stay away.

This introduces that second hurdle referred to earlier. While it is very common, it is far from universal. This hurdle appears when the young congregation seems to have grown beyond the capability of the organization to assimilate and service the new members. In part this is a conflict between the "pioneers" and the "homesteaders" and their differing agendas. In part it is the combination of an inability of the meaningful small groups mentioned earlier to absorb newcomers into meaningful membership and a failure to form additional new small groups with the passing of years. This pattern can be seen in the young congregation which begins to level off in size and then to decline. As this happens longtime members move away and replacements are assimilated at a slower pace. The quality of the effort to create and maintain meaningful small groups declines because the creation of each additional small group in those early days means the quantity of resources to create and maintain additional new groups has diminished. The creation and care of small groups require resources. As these groups are created the young church often finds itself short of these necessary resources. The church is not able to help existing groups assimilate newcomers or to create additional new groups within the congregation.

Westminster Church was fortunate in not falling over this obstacle. One reason it did not trip over this hurdle was the effective emphasis on the health of the group life of the congregation described earlier. A second reason was expressed in the lament of the pastor who commented one day, "One of our biggest problems has been the high turnover of the membership. This is a very mobile community. You may not believe this, but it's true. When we celebrated our fifth anniversary only twelve of the original ninety-one charter members were still on the resident member roll and when we celebrated our tenth anniversary that number had shrunk to five! For anyone to expect a congregation to continue to grow in the face of that kind of mobility requires a belief in miracles."

This comment can be filed under either of two clichés: "Every cloud has a silver lining" or "Growth means trading one set of problems for a different set of problems."

Pastoral Tenure

A third and perhaps the most common pitfall encountered by the young congregation is the interruption in direction and continuity following a change of ministers. This usually is most highly visible and destructive in the congregation which has had five to seven ministers with an average tenure of three or four years during its first twenty-one years of life. There are several dimensions to this issue. One is the general pattern which suggests that *from a congregational perspective* the most productive years for the typical pastorate are years five, six, seven, and eight. The minister who moves on after three or four years deprives his congregation of what often potentially could be the most productive and effective years of his ministry in that place. A second facet of this issue relates to the tendency for a new congregation to level off prematurely on a relatively low plateau in size. Introducing a new professional leader every three or four years reinforces this tendency and appears to have been a significant factor in the number of new congregations which today often are described as "arrested development problems." A third facet of this issue is the more subjective question of how a new congregation moves from a survival and goal-oriented era of its life into a new definition of identity and role. (This issue is described in more detail in chapter nine.) Frequent changes in pastors tend to interrupt or divert this transformation. Finally, the frequent turnover of pastors may cause many members to drop into inactivity if each new minister brings with him his own definition of the purpose and role of the church in the world today and seeks to impose that on the membership. If three or four successive ministers have sharply differing views on this, it is easy for dedicated and active lay leaders to find other less bewildering and frustrating channels outside this young congregation through which they can express their commitment to Jesus Christ. This problem was completely avoided at Westminster when the first pastor remained for fourteen years. That exceptionally long tenure for a minister, however, created two other obstacles which will be described later.

Straight-Line Projections

A fourth very common hurdle encountered by many young congregations almost did trip the people at Westminster Church. This is the tendency of many people, including demographers, church planners, economists, pastors, denominational executives, and lay leaders to rely too heavily on straight-line projections. In the youthful congregation this appears as a straight-line projection of the growth figures of the first five or six years in planning the size and cost of the meeting place. While straight-line projections have fallen into disfavor all across society in recent years, thanks to the contributions of such original thinkers as Peter Drucker and others, thousands of young congregations have overbuilt and have felt obligated to redefine the purpose of their congregation as primarily that of raising money to meet debt service charges.

At Westminster, however, the straight-line projection method was used. After the first building was completed, planning began on the second unit. By the end of its first five years Westminster had grown to include 475 confirmed members on the active roll. On the basis of this, an average *net* increase of 95 members per year, plans were prepared for two more building programs. These were based on projections which estimated the membership at 660 by the end of 1960, 1,200 by the end of 1965, and 2,000 by December, 1970. These projections were the basis for both building design and for planning the method of financing the new buildings. The second unit consisting of offices, additional church school rooms, and one very large room which would serve as a temporary worship facility and eventually would be converted into a fellowship hall, was completed in 1959. By that time the membership had climbed to 648, and the earlier projections appeared to be validated.

While the membership growth pattern of the 1960s did not keep up with the earlier projections, in 1962 the congregation made the decision to go ahead with the construction of the third unit which was to include a 700-seat permanent worship facility, additional restrooms, a church parlor, and a new set of offices to accommodate a professional staff of four plus secretarial staff and a workroom. The building fund was a disappointment since the pledges were only 90 percent of the goal. The lowest bid was $77,000 above the architect's estimate. After eighteen months of indecision and reworking the plans, the congregation by a 431 to 147 vote decided to go ahead with a revised design which reduced the size of the project to a sanctuary seating 480 plus a forty-member choir. The proposed new office suite was reduced to accommodate three professional members and two secretaries, and the parlor was eliminated. Ground was broken in September, 1965, and the new structure was opened for use on Thanksgiving Sunday in 1966.

In mid-1967 the first pastor left to take a position as a staff member in a regional judicatory of the denomination. One of the reasons he left was because of two earlier unhappy experiences with assistant ministers—a subject which merits more detailed discussion later in this chapter. A more significant reason, perhaps, was that while Westminster continued to show an increase in the total membership year after year, the average net gain dropped from 95 in the earlier years to 47 in 1962, 39 in 1963, 31 in 1964, 19 in 1965, and 12 in 1966. When this first pastor left, the confirmed membership figure stood at 933, well below the projection of 1,200 by 1965 and not at all promising in regard to the target of 2,000 confirmed members by 1970. "Perhaps a new face in the pulpit and a new voice at board meetings will help produce a new surge of interest among the people at Westminster," commented the pastor as he explained his decision to leave Westminster and to accept this new position.

What happened next?

To condense a long and very complex story into one sentence, Westminster found itself with seven years of bad luck. Or, to be more analytical, during the 1960s Westminster encountered a series of obstacles very common to young congregations moving toward their mature years. Perhaps the best way to describe these is to resume the discussion of these hurdles, obstacles, and pitfalls.

That First Assistant!

A fifth pitfall in the path of many rapidly growing young congregations was illustrated by Westminster in the early 1960s. Two years after completion of the second unit in the building program the membership had passed the 700 mark and the Sunday morning worship attendance averaged 325. It was decided that a second professional person should be secured to help the pastor carry this increasingly heavy ministerial load. In September, 1961, a young man, who had just completed his seminary training, came to be the second minister on the staff of Westminster Church. His special responsibilities were (naturally!) to be Christian education and youth work. While no one saw this in these terms, he also came to be the second minister in a situation in which all of the people, both lay and clergy, had been trained and had trained each other to function with the leadership focus on a unit consisting of *one* minister and a number of lay persons. Few significant organizational changes were made and absolutely no retraining of this old leadership unit was undertaken. The almost inevitable result was an increase in unhappiness because of the friction and tension. After twenty months this assistant minister departed. He left frustrated and the congregation felt cheated. Westminster fell into this trap twice.

In the normal, natural, and very human (but not necessarily very healthy) approach to an unhappy situation the departure of the first young minister provoked a search for scapegoats. Two were quickly identified. The obvious one was this young minister who "didn't understand his role," "wanted to take over the church," "could relate to the youth, but couldn't get along with their parents," "wanted to preach all of the time," and "was lazy, he simply hadn't had the opportunity to learn how to work." The more compassionate and sophisticated leaders were reluctant to fall into the trap of placing all the blame for this unfortunate experience on the inexperienced young minister. They concluded that the real fault was with the theological seminaries "which don't take the time or don't have the ability to train students to serve in a staff role or to function effectively as assistant or associate ministers."

This subject came up again a few months after the second assistant minister had been asked to resign. On this occasion a group of leaders was discussing program planning with an outside consultant. After hearing these two tales of woe, the consultant asked the chairman of the program planning committee, an attorney, two questions.

"In your practice of law, do you handle divorce cases?"

"Yes, a great many," was the reply.

"How often have you handled a divorce case in which 100 percent of the blame for the failure of that marriage rested with one party?"

"Never," replied the chairman of the program planning committee.

Hidden Building Costs

During these years Westminster encountered a sixth pitfall that traps the vast majority of young congregations, regardless of size. This is the hidden cost of constructing a new building.[1]

As described earlier, Westminster spent approximately four and one-half years between the time of the first decision to go ahead with construction of the third unit and completion of that structure. Thus with the planning that preceded the 1962 decision to go ahead, the obvious costs included five years of time plus the time and energy that went into the capital funds campaigns plus the actual construction cost of $325,000. There were several other less obvious costs.

One of these hidden costs was the product of (1) the two unhappy experiences with two young assistant ministers and (2) the financial squeeze resulting from construction costs larger than estimated and the disappointing results of the first capital funds drive for financing this third unit. The combination of these two factors led to the decision to postpone the replacement of the second assistant minister. This decision can be translated into either of these two statements, "Let's finance a part of the cost of the new building out of the salary we won't pay a second minister," or "Let's trade our building financing problem for a different problem and hope we are trading up in the process."

[1] For the other side of this issue concerning the "fringe benefits" which may accompany a building program, see Lyle E. Schaller, *The Local Church Looks to the Future* (Nashville: Abingdon Press, 1968), pp. 144-155.

Another way to describe this particular hidden cost is to recount what happened at Westminster. The average attendance at worship climbed year after year and eventually passed the 250 mark. This is one indicator of the maximum work load for one pastor with an excellent full-time secretary. As the worship attendance continued to climb, a second minister was called to help the pastor carry the load. This arrangement frequently does not prove satisfactory the first time. At Westminster it was an unhappy experience twice. This, combined with the financial squeeze caused by the building program, produced the decision, initiated by the pastor at Westminster as is so often the case, to go ahead with only one professional staff member.

While the membership total continued to rise, the size of the congregation as measured by the worship attendance dwindled. Eventually it dropped to the maximum that could be served by one overworked full-time minister.

To shift from Westminster to a more general description, this pattern, which occurs time after time, can be described in these terms. To the outsider it appears the congregation grows to a size which is (1) beyond the work load capability of one minister and (2) not as comfortable from the perspective of the members as back when it was smaller and everyone knew everyone else. When the young congregation reaches this size, it appears in retrospect, there is an unconscious, unintentional, and undeliberate effort by the members to cut it back down to a more comfortable size which can be served by one clergyman. This is relatively easy to accomplish as active leaders move away and are replaced by unassimilated newcomers, as the number leaving may begin to approach or even to exceed the number coming in, as people in the middle circle of involvement drift out to an outer circle of less involvement, and as the people on the periphery drift into almost complete inactivity.

At this point the young congregation is faced with two choices. One is to attempt to halt the decline and maintain the size at around 200 at worship on an average Sunday morning. The other, and far more difficult, choice is to make a self-conscious and intentional decision to be a *large* congregation with a very *complex* organizational structure involving two or three full-time professional staff members, a more complex Sunday morning schedule which completely eliminates even the dream of "our becoming one big family gathered together every Sunday morning to worship God," and accepting a role as a congregation of congregations based on a positive affirmation of pluralism and diversity. This appears to be the place at which a great many youthful, and also several older congregations find themselves when confronted with the opportunity for continued growth in size. The acceptance of organizational complexity and the affirmation of diversity are the two most critical issues. A distant third is the staff question.

At Westminster one of the hidden costs of the third unit was a decline *in the rate* of membership growth and an actual decline in worship attendance as the staff was cut back in size in order to finance the new building.

Another hidden cost of that third unit at Westminster was in the adult Sunday school. When Westminster celebrated its ninth birthday in 1962, the Sunday school included six strong and vigorous adult classes which could have been used as models for meaningful small groups within the Sunday church school. By 1969, although the membership of the congregation had increased during these seven years, there were only three adult classes in the Sunday church school at Westminster. Why?

The most frequently heard explanations were, "The Sunday school is in trouble all over," "Adults simply aren't interested in Sunday school the way they used to be," "Television," and "People here don't know one another the way they used to, so it's hard to develop the loyalties that once were so strong here."

From an outsider's perspective it appears that the adult Sunday school was hurt by (1) a diversion of the time and energy of several key persons who had been influential adult class leaders from their Sunday school classes to the complexities of the prolonged building program, (2) the lack of staff support as the pastor also was caught up in the building planning game and effective staff replacements to help with program responsibilities were not available, (3) the departure in 1967 of the first pastor who had been very effective in the formation and nurture of small groups, (4) the adult classes which had been effective points for the reception and assimilation of new members ceased to fulfill this role, (5) new members, especially able male leaders, were assimilated via the various committees concerned with the building and did not have the need, time, or energy to be active members of an adult class, (6) the emergence, to a minor degree, of the "pioneers" versus the "home-steaders" division described earlier, (7) some of the key leaders who were part of the glue holding these classes together in earlier years moved away and were not replaced, and (8) the reward system at Westminster shifted from a recognition of leadership skills in program and ministry to an emphasis on leadership skills in building planning, construction, and financing.

Perhaps the most serious hidden cost of the building program at Westminster did not appear until several years later. It can be described most clearly by shifting the focus of this narrative from Westminster to another congregation.

After the Wolf Is Gone?

While it is seventh in an account of the pitfalls that may be found in the path of the young congregation as it moves toward maturity, this issue ranks among the first two or three in terms of frequency and seriousness. It can be described as a subversion of goals or by asking, "What do we do after we've paid off the mortgage?" or "What is a goal?" Perhaps the best way to introduce the subject is to quote a section from the annual report to his congregation by the Reverend Charles Lee Wilson.

We built a new building and we agreed to make payments of $1,900 each and every month for a long period of time —and some of us spoke of that payment that always followed us as the "wolf."

Some months we fell behind in our payments and we felt the wolf snapping at our heels, but every year as the wolf followed up and down our monthly hills and valleys we would put on a blinding burst of speed and close our year panting gratefully, "We made it again!"

Somewhere along the years, we said, "We have lived with this wolf so closely and so long that we ought to make a pet of him." However, it wasn't until we finished the debt and said, "farewell to you, wolf" that we realized what a likable pet he really was. He gave us *direction*—like, "which way shall we go?—here comes the wolf—let's go to the closest spot to find a payment." He gave us *motivation*—"man, we've got to make another payment or we are in trouble with the wolf." The wolf also gave us a wonderful excuse for anything we didn't get around to—if it took time, money, or action, we could whiz by saying, "I made my payment and my business is staying ahead of the wolf."

For so long, we could hate the wolf, blame the wolf, enjoy beating the wolf, tell each other scary wolf stories and everything—right up until we paid the mortgage and waved farewell to the wolf. We paid off the mortgage with such enthusiasm that we had $3,000 left over. We might have done it a year ago, but we got a new organ and bought a lot instead. The $10,000 payment on the total purchase price of the lot was sort of like a wolf cub—cute and a little like daddy. In fact, when we got through with the debt and had $3,000 left, we gave it all to the lot so the "little wolf" would be two years ahead of his diet.

105

Every active church member has heard in one form or another the comment, "Isn't it true that a church does its best when it has a mortgage to pay off?" Or sometimes the comment is offered with a trace of nostalgia, "Back when we were in the midst of our building program, enthusiasm was high and we had more participation by more members than we have ever had since. Maybe we should start another building program?" Occasionally the comment is made in a voice filled with regret. "I thought that when we finally got the new building completed and the debt paid off we would be free to go about our business of being the church. But instead of interest and enthusiasm going up, it's been on a steady decline ever since the day we made the final payment on the mortgage! Why?"

These comments represent other forms of the wolf story. Each one refers back to when a congregation was being pursued by a wolf. Together they illustrate several of the basic factors in parish planning.

The first lesson is the definition of a goal. Too often the goals formulated in the parish are really wishes, not goals. "Our goal for this year is to improve our ministry to youth."

"That's important," adds someone else, "but I believe our number one goal for the coming year should be to do more for the elderly."

These are not goals, they are wishes or dreams! At best they are suggestions on setting the priorities among the goals.

By definition a goal is something which you can tell when it has been reached. Staying a jump or two ahead of a hungry wolf is a goal. By definition and to be operationally useful a goal should be *specific*. Staying out ahead of that hungry wolf who is snapping at your heels is a specific goal. "Having better church school facilities" is a dream. Completing the construction of a new building is a specific goal. "Having more room for the children to play outdoors"

106

is a dream. Purchasing the lot next door to the church for $20,000 is a specific goal. A goal also should be *achievable*. Staying ahead of that pursuing wolf is an achievable goal, although at times, and especially at the beginning of the chase, some may doubt it. Keeping up-to-date on the monthly payments on the mortgage is an achievable goal. A goal also should be *measurable*. It is possible to measure the gap between us and that pursuing wolf. It is possible to measure the progress being made in constructing the new building or in paying off the mortgage. A goal should be *visible*. We can see how we are doing in staying ahead of that wolf and we can see how wide the gap is. We can see the progress on the new church building every time we come to our congregational meeting place. We can see the numbers of our remaining indebtedness grow smaller with each monthly payment on the mortgage.

These are the four essential elements of a goal. They represent the difference between a wish or a dream and a goal. They also are representative of the early goals of the young congregation.

The second lesson illustrated by this story of the wolf is the vulnerability of institutions to a subversion of goals. In this process a goal which is adopted as a means to an end becomes an end in itself. Building a meeting place to enable people to come together to hear the preaching of the Word, for the administration of the sacraments, and for the other ministries of the church is a means to an end. Too often, however, the planning, construction, financing, and care of the new building becomes an end in itself. The purpose of the congregation is subverted from its original reason for being into completing the building and paying off the mortgage. Staying ahead of the wolf becomes the name of the game. Whenever the means to an end becomes a substitute for the end itself or for the basic purpose of the group or organization, the door is opened for disillusionment, gloom, and apathy.

A third lesson is that it applies not only to the congregation as a whole, but also to every organization and group within the parish. The women's organization thrives in the church when it has a clearly defined purpose that is compatible with the nature of the church. When the goals are specific, achievable, measurable, and visible, enthusiasm usually is high. When the monthly meeting is held because the group has always had monthly meetings, apathy begins to surface. When the original purpose of the group is redefined to place most or all of the emphasis on "fellowship," interest declines. When new members are sought only in the interests of perpetuating the organization, few knock on the door for admission.

This same pattern can be seen in the adult Sunday school classes, in the youth group, and in every other organization in the parish. When the goals are clear, when the wolf is in pursuit and providing motivation and direction, enthusiasm runs high. When the wolf dies or goes away and when the mortgage finally is paid off or when the goal has been achieved, enthusiasm declines and participation drops off. The excitement is in staying ahead of the wolf—in the doing, not in reminiscing over the chase or in reliving the past.

A fourth lesson illustrated here is the broad sense of ownership of the goal. When the wolf is in pursuit, everyone shares the goal of staying ahead of that hungry animal! Likewise enthusiasm is highest in the parish when as many people as possible feel a sense of ownership of the major goals. Most church leaders realize that when it comes to the vote on a building program, it is desirable to postpone the decision a month or two in order to win more supporters for the program. A 113 to 0 vote is tremendously more helpful than a 68 to 45 vote when the proposal reaches the implementation stage.

Another lesson in this story of the wolf is in the many potential congregational victories. Every month and every year that congregation celebrated its success in staying ahead of the wolf. Each of these victories provided a psychic reward for the members struggling to pay off that debt. The parish without goals offers fewer satisfactions or psychic rewards as compensation for the volunteers. This is another source of the apathy which often sets in following completion of a major project, such as a building program, which has provided a variety of satisfactions for many people.

Finally, this story illustrates very graphically the value of self-evaluation. Every month the members could measure the gap between themselves and that wolf. This self-evaluation process affected subsequent performance!

Here again a building program or the repayment of a mortgage offer clear examples of an essential element of a good goal, a built-in process for self-evaluation which is useful to people as they determine what must be done next.

What happens when the wolf goes away, when the new building is completed, or when the mortgage is finally retired? This is the point at which planning proves its value. The parish with a sense of intentionality can avoid depending on the wolf for direction and motivation. The parish which emphasizes purpose can avoid the subversive pressures to substitute the means to an end for the end itself. The parish with a sense of ministry and mission can avoid the "post-building blues." How?

The answer to that one word question is contained in the story of the wolf. The continuing goals of the parish should:

1. Be directly related to the central purpose of the church.
2. Be related to the available and potential resources of the parish.
3. Be specific, achievable, measurable, and have high visibility.

4. Be phrased in terms so that everyone can easily see the direction and the progress which is being made in achieving the goal.
5. Include both long-term goals and short-term goals. (The short-term goals are especially important in strengthening the self-confidence of the congregation during that period when it may appear that progress is very slow toward achieving large, long-term goals.)
6. Be developed with as broad a base of "ownership" as possible.
7. Include in the process of formulating the goals the people who will be responsible for implementation.
8. Be scheduled so that when one big and exciting goal has been achieved or completed, other goals already have been formulated and are in the process of being implemented. (The "postbuilding blues" and the apathy that often sets in following repayment of the debt are in part the result of a shift from a goal-oriented parish to a goalless congregation.)
9. Take into account the value of providing "satisfactions" and a sense of movement and progress for all of the members of the parish.
10. Include some yardsticks or standards for continuing self-evaluation by parish leaders.

Making this shift from staying ahead of the wolf to ministry-oriented goals is a pitfall that traps many a young congregation just when the members breathe a sigh of relief that the long chase to stay ahead of the wolf has ended.

One Service or Two?

One of the most divisive issues to arise during the 1960s at Westminster was a product of the building program. It is such a common problem that it can be identified as the eighth in this list of pitfalls and hurdles.

For several months following completion of the second unit back in 1959 Westminster had been able to return to the earlier practice of one worship service on Sunday morning. By the late winter of 1960, however, the continued growth of the congregation forced a return to two services. There simply was not sufficient room with only one service.

Many of the members regretted this return to two services. While they recognized the necessity of the decision and acknowledged the lack of any alternative, they saw it as a divisive action. Therefore, these members looked forward to the completion of the third unit and assumed that when the sanctuary was completed, it would enable Westminster to return to the pattern of one worship on Sunday morning.

The various arguments offered in the summer and fall of 1966 in favor of returning to the practice of only one worship service on Sunday morning could be summarized in two frequently repeated comments: "There's plenty of room in the new building to accommodate everyone. Why did we build this if we're not going to make use of it?" and "I can understand some of the reasons why we should continue a schedule of two Sunday morning worship services, and I can see why some people believe this would be a good idea, but I'm opposed! If we continue with two services, we may increase the total attendance slightly, but that advantage is offset by the fact that we will make the present split a permanent division in this congregation!"

That first statement can be translated very simply, Now that we have a new building, let's encourage the building to dictate the schedule. This condition is most visible in those congregations with a building designed to seat 600 for worship and one service with an average attendance of 250. All proposals to offer people a greater range of choices in time and worship style are rejected "because the building won't let us do that." The building, by its size and design, demands that there be only the one worship service on Sunday morning and that it follow the traditional format with a very passive role for the congregation.

Westminster, like many other congregations which planned a permanent worship facility in the early 1960s based on straight-line projections of growth and a traditional worship pattern, produced a structure which demanded the role of master rather than of servant.

The second comment about dividing the congregation is nonsense! When the new structure was completed in the fall of 1966, Westminster counted approximately 920 names on the confirmed membership roll. The average attendance at worship had peaked at 350 in 1962 and then had dropped slowly back to 225 during that period of unrest which led to the forced resignation of the second assistant minister. It then climbed back up to 275 by the time the new building was completed in the fall of 1966. (With adequate professional staff it would have been reasonable to expect the worship attendance in this thirteen-year-old, 920-member congregation to have averaged at least 350 to 400 in the fall of 1966. As was pointed out earlier, however, the decision at Westminster had been to finance part of the cost of the new building out of the salary not paid a second minister, a "saving" this congregation could ill afford.)

An attendance survey for the five Sundays of October, 1966, when the worship attendance averaged 273, revealed that 529 confirmed members attended at least once. More specifically, 72 confirmed members attended all five Sundays, 83 attended four times, 54 attended three Sundays, 113 were there twice in October, and 187 attended only once. There was an average of eight visitors and twelve children of preconfirmation age at worship each Sunday that month.

How can these figures be interpreted in the light of the second comment favoring a return to one Sunday morning worship service?

First, during this last month before the new building was completed and when excitement was comparatively high, nearly 400 confirmed members stayed away from both worship services every Sunday. This suggests that instead of worrying about a division within that group of 500 who attended at least once, a higher priority should have been a concern over the nearly 400 who stayed away completely for at least five consecutive Sundays. The congregation already was split three ways—a large group who regularly stayed away from worship, a group about one-half that size who attended regularly, and a third group of 300 who attended irregularly.

Second, the statistical evidence suggests that instead of reducing the range of opportunities available to people to come together to worship God, the choices should be enlarged.

Third, instead of falling into the temptation to blame those 400 members who did not attend even once, it might be more helpful for the leaders and decision-makers at Westminster to ask themselves, "What are we doing or not doing to cause people, who apparently united with this congregation in good faith, to stay away from the corporate worship of God?"

Finally, these attendance figures lead to a discussion of another issue which often creates problems for those young congregations which grow so rapidly that the congregation as a body is not able to stay in touch with the membership.

Internal Communication

This ninth pitfall is in part a product of other hazards and in part a result of the increasing size of the young congregation. In its first few years of life the young congregation typically depends on a simple and highly informal internal communication system, and it works. This is a characteristic of the meaningful small group where there are many opportunities for face-to-face communication. As the young congregation grows in size, as the groups multiply in number, and as a larger proportion of members are less frequently and less deeply involved, the quality of internal communication deteriorates. People *do* respond to that which they are aware of and *do not* respond to that which they are not aware of in the life of the church. Thus, the deterioration of the quality of the internal communication often is wrongly diagnosed as a lack of responsiveness or a decline in interest among the members rather than as a decline in the quality of internal communication.

As the young congregation moves into maturity, it is of critical importance that the quality of internal communication not be allowed to deteriorate. Among other requirements this means an increase in the number of different channels used for communication and a more systematic effort to maintain more face-to-face communications. It appears that at Westminster an excessive reliance had been placed on the calling program carried on by members of the governing board, and this was one (but only one of several) reasons why the internal communication system was malfunctioning. A system that had worked very effectively in the early years of a much smaller congregation was beginning to wear out. (This also illustrates one of the key issues in an understaffed congregation. The usual procedure is to ask, "If we did add a second minister, what would he or she do?" A much more incisive question is, "In this understaffed situation, what is not getting done?" The work that does *not* get done is often what seriously harms the young and growing congregation. At Westminster this could be seen in the deterioration of the calling responsibilities of members of the governing board, in the decline in worship attendance from the peak of 350, in the inadequate internal communication system, in the decay of the adult Sunday school classes, in a deterioration of the health of the group life of the

114

congregation, in the decrease in the rate of accessions to the membership roll and in the failure to adequately assimilate many of the newer "homesteaders.")

Closely related to these two issues of the attendance-to-membership ratio and the adequacy of the internal communication system is a tenth pitfall that automatically goes with the franchise of being a relatively young and rapidly growing congregation. It usually moves from a concern to becoming a divisive issue after the second pastor has arrived on the scene, after the congregation has passed the 500 or 600 level in membership, after the beginning of the second decade of the young congregation's life, and after the congregation has become a comparatively heterogeneous collection of individuals and families as contrasted with the comparatively homogeneous large group in the earlier years.

Pastoral Visitation

Perhaps the most highly visible characteristic of the congregation which has moved from youth to maturity is reflected in the comments, "It used to be our minister did a lot more calling than he does now." Or "In the old days our pastor used to drop in on us three or four times a year, now he never comes by the house unless someone is ill or there is an emergency or a special need."

As the new congregation grows in size and complexity and as the prospective member to be visited becomes a member who is met in church, the demands on the minister's time for administration, committee meetings, and counseling continue to climb and a diminishing amount of time is available for pastoral calling in the home.

At Westminster, as in many other large, complex, urban, and understaffed congregations, it may be helpful to define the context more carefully. For many

115

people pastoral calling and home visitation appear to be used as synonyms. More realistically the two should be viewed as separate subjects. At Westminster, as in many similar congregations the minister made a huge number of "pastoral calls" every month—in his sermons; before, during and after meetings; at the hospitals; when people dropped by the church building; on a variety of occasions on Sunday morning; by appointment; and on other planned and unplanned occasions.

This meant there was considerable "pastoral calling" on the more active one-half of the membership, but comparatively little on the least active one-half. The general oversight of the membership was further inhibited by a system which (1) expected the members of the governing board to visit every member-household (shotgun approach) rather than to concentrate on the least active one-third (rifle approach) and (2) appears not to have been especially effective in reaching the total membership.

What is the answer to this almost universal issue of pastoral calling? The most common response is to scapegoat. One (or is it a thousand?) congregation had a minister who was an extraordinarily effective preacher, but who was somewhat introverted, aloof, and rarely called. When he resigned, the pulpit committee was instructed to find a "warm pastoral type who loves people and hopefully is an acceptable preacher." They found exactly the minister they were seeking. After four years he resigned because he no longer could tolerate the unending comments about his predecessor's excellent preaching. Perhaps a more creative approach is to change the frame of reference and shift from pastoral visitation to the care of the members.

Those Blinking Red Lights

On a recent trip I came back to the motel late in the evening. The first thing I saw when I opened the door to my dark room was a blinking red light. This was a signal to call the desk. The desk clerk responded to my call by informing me that someone had left an envelope for me at the desk.

The next evening, before going to my room, I stopped at the desk to inquire if there were any messages for me. There were two. When I reached my room, the red light was not blinking.

Many motels have similar systems to inform guests there are messages for them at the desk. There is the need for a similar system in every congregation!

Create in your imagination, if you will please, a large electrical board similar to those used as signal lights in motel rooms. Each bulb represents one person in the congregation. Some of these bulbs are blinking. Several have been blinking on and off for so long the bulbs are burned out. Others were blinking recently, but are not lighted now. A few are blinking, but no one appears to be aware of that fact.

What is the system used to discover the content of the messages being signaled by those blinking red lights? The larger the congregation, the greater the probability that many of these red lights have been blinking without a response for a long time.

Before moving on to a description of several responses to this situation, three basic points must be made.

First, *if none of the leaders believe there are any red lights blinking, nothing can be done about it!*

Second, there is an important difference between getting these lights turned off and receiving the messages waiting to be transmitted.

Third, the existence of those blinking red lights represents both the existence of some concerns and also the cause of other problems.

Different parishes respond in different ways to the existence of these blinking red lights. One of the most creative requires keeping a record of the church attendance of all members. Whenever a person who is a regular attender misses Sunday morning worship three times in a row, this is seen as a blinking red light and a call is made to discover why. Likewise, when a person who attends only occasionally is present for three consecutive Sundays, it is assumed this represents a blinking red light and a call is made.

Perhaps the most widespread response to the blinking red lights has been and still is pastoral calling. As a part of his routine of calling on people in their homes, at their places of employment, on the golf course, and in casual conversations in scores of other situations the pastor discovers many blinking red lights that he had not known were lighted. This type of response to the issue is less common than it once was. There are many reasons for this, including television, the increasing geographical separation of the place of residence and the place of worship, the competition of other activities for people's time which makes them less accessible, the change in the definition of role for many ministers, the pressure of institutional concerns on the pastor's schedule, and a score of other factors.

This decline in routine calling by the pastor has left a vacuum which must be filled in one way or another. In some congregations an "under shepherd" or "neighborhood unit" plan has been developed which places the responsibility on each of several lay persons to watch for blinking red lights among the ten to twenty households under their care. At Westminster this responsibility was placed on the already overworked members of the governing board. While it can be a very effective response this system tends to break down after the first year unless it receives careful and continuing maintenance.

Another widely discussed approach is to form a series of "caring groups" with the expectation that (1) every member of the congregation will be a part of one of these groups and (2) the members of the group will develop into a caring fellowship which will both discover and respond to every blinking red light within that fellowship. This, too, has the limitation that rarely are more than one-half of the members involved in active caring groups. At Westminster this was a very helpful approach for about eight years.

Many congregations plan a series of "cottage meetings" each year. Each cottage meeting is held in the home of a member of the parish and somewhere between ten and twenty other members are invited in for the evening. Every member of the congregation receives an invitation to one of these cottage meetings and the entire evening, sometimes even two or three evenings, is devoted to listening for the messages that those present want to transmit to their church leaders. In terms of the expenditure of time, this is one of the most efficient responses to those blinking red lights. The major shortcoming is that typically one-fourth to two-thirds of the members do not attend a cottage meeting.

One of the most widely used responses is in the thousands of congregations where the leaders guess at which bulbs are lighted and speculate on the content of the messages waiting to be transmitted. A closely related approach is in those congregations where there is a response only to those blinking red lights which either (1) are accompanied by the blast of a siren or (2) represent an "important" member. The rest of the lights continue to blink until the bulb burns out. This approach is remarkably effective in reducing a larger congregation to a manageable size. It was used at Westminster from 1962 to 1970. It often is used in those congregations which traditionally have depended on the pastor to discover and respond to all blinking red lights, but this cannot be done either because of the definition of the role of the clergy and/or because the size of the congregation is beyond the capability of the ministerial staff to carry out this responsibility without help.

Another approach to this issue of the blinking red

lights is being used by an increasing number of congregations and can be described simply as "the two-call listening system."

In a five-hundred-member congregation consisting of two hundred households, for example, forty calling "units" will be recruited and trained. Each unit consists either of a person who is able and willing to call alone or a team of two persons who will call together. Typically this means a total of sixty callers. The callers "contract" to make two calls at each of five households. This also means each caller is called on by someone else. Every household is visited.

In larger congregations with more than six or seven hundred members it may not be possible to find enough callers to call at every household. A common pattern in these larger congregations is to call at every other household this year and the alternate households the following year.

The first call is strictly a "listening" call. After a period of time for introductions and building rapport, the caller inquires, "How are things going with you? We recognize that a lot of people have complaints, suggestions, creative ideas, hurts, and other concerns which are not always heard. As we have become more aware of the fact that the concerns of many people are not being heard, it was decided to undertake this effort to call at every home in the parish. We're calling it 'Operation Listening Post,' and we want to be as sure as we can that everyone has a chance to be heard. What are your ideas, concerns, gripes, suggestions, or comments? I'm here to listen."

In the typical congregation close to one-half of the time the caller finds that simply pushing the "on" button with such an introductory statement releases a flood of comments. In the other one-half of the calls the person or people being called on have learned to be very polite, reserved, or guarded when talking about themselves or about their church. In these cases the caller has to be much more patient and persistent. This often requires a willingness to sit through long periods of silence waiting for the other person to speak and an ability to "prime the pump."

In these calls it is of critical importance that the caller not lapse into an interview by asking a series of specific questions such as "How do you like the worship service?" or "How do you feel about the church school?" When the time comes to "prime the pump," this can be done by "playing back" what has just been said to make sure the caller heard correctly what was said—by asking the basic introductory question over again in another form or by simply asking, "What else is there you would like to comment about?" The question should always be nondirective and open-ended.

It also is of vital importance that the caller listens and only listens! The caller should not feel obligated to correct misstatements of fact or to respond to questions which may reverse the roles with the caller being interviewed by the resident. The caller also should not feel defensive about critical comments or respond either affirmatively or negatively to criticisms about the church. This requires considerable restraint on the part of most callers. For some active and very loyal members this borders on the impossible!

The role of the callers in this round of calls can be compared to a sponge or to a blotter. A good blotter will absorb green ink, black ink, red ink, and blue ink. The role of the caller is to be an active listener, but this does not necssarily mean a highly vocal listener. This means the caller both hears *and remembers* what is heard. Frequently after several minutes the caller may feel obligated to explain, "Please understand every comment you make will be treated as anonymous. This means your name will not be attached to anything you say. It is important, however, that the substance of your comments be heard, so this cannot be treated as confidential. I will report on what I hear from all of my calls, but no one will ever know who said what. What you have to say is important, and therefore it must be fed in to how we make plans for the nature, direction, and planning of the ministry of our church."

While some people will have only one or two or three comments to offer, others may have several. In these calls the visitor may want to say something like this, "You're raising a series of very important issues and questions. Do you mind if I make a few notes so I won't forget any of this?" It may be at this point the caller will want to press the distinction between anonymity and confidentiality. It is essential for the entire process that every caller remember every suggestion, complaint, constructive idea, question, gripe, or compliment. This requires making a list for each visit, either during the call or immediately afterward.

After each caller has completed the assignment of five calls, it is necessary to report back what was heard. One of the most widely used methods is to schedule two or three sharing sessions in which the visitors are invited to come to one of these sessions and share with one another their experiences and what they have heard.

A variation of this is to ask all members of the governing body of the congregation to meet without any agenda except to hear the reporting back from the callers.

Another approach is to ask each visitor to fill out a one-page report form for each call.

Which is the best approach to use? Perhaps a combination of two or three in order to give each volunteer caller a choice in reporting back. If you use a report form, ask the visitors to fill out one form for *each* call.

After all the feedback from these calls has been processed by the leadership groups of the parish, the second round of calls can be made.

These are very easy and usually very enjoyable calls for the visitors to make. The primary purpose of this second call is to "prove" that the people called on during the first round of calls were heard. Thus the callers return to the same homes they had visited and review each of the questions, suggestions, complaints, or proposals which had been raised in the earlier call. "When I was here two months ago you raised a question about why the parking lot had not been paved. Several others raised the same point, and this is what has happened."

Sometimes the caller has nothing positive to report on any of the six or eight comments heard earlier. How does the typical member respond to this? Frequently with the comment, "Golly, you listened to what I had to say far more carefully than I did!" When this is translated into operational English, it comes out, "Well, I really am more interested in having my point of view heard than I am in whether anything is done about it right away. Until you came along a couple of months ago, I was pretty well convinced that nobody paid any attention to how I felt or what I have to say." For many people it is far more important to be heard than to be heeded!

Churches which have used this system have found many benefits resulting from it. As emphasized earlier, the messages which are symbolized by those blinking red lights are transmitted, heard, considered and, when appropriate, acted on in developing the total program and ministry of that cogregation. The second call is necessary to "prove" that the message was received. This is the primary and central reason for undertaking this approach.

In addition, there are many fringe benefits. Members become better acquainted with one another. New friendships are formed. Lonely people are discovered. The leaders and decision-makers who call have new firsthand data for the decision-making processes. New needs are identified. New and useful ideas and suggestions are received. Church attendance usually climbs during each round of calls.

Legitimate complaints are heard. The participation base is broadened. Calling becomes redefined as fun rather than as a chore.

For the congregation contemplating this type of visitation program there are several caution signs which should be noted.

1. The most widespread difficulty encountered by congregations who try this system is the result of past training. In many congregations the members have been trained that no one from their church calls on them except (a) when there is a death in the family, (b) during a serious illness, (c) to seek volunteers for church work, and (d) to ask for money. In these congregations the callers often have difficulty in convincing people that someone from the church is interested simply in listening to what they have to say!

2. In developing the list of five calls for each caller (or calling team) to visit, include a cross section of members. Do *not* have anyone call only on five inactive members or on five very active families.

3. Try to make sure that *every* caller has at least two calls that will be easy or pleasant or rewarding visits. Experience suggests that, on the average, out of every five calls, three will be surprisingly (to the caller) easy, pleasant, and rewarding; one will be neutral; and one will be on the negative side of the line.

4. Select the callers by invitation. Do not issue a general invitation for volunteers! Some people have gifts which greatly reduce their effectiveness as listeners!

5. No one should go out to call until after first being trained in effective listening or "active listening" skills.

6. If all of the leaders know the major issue that will come up on most calls, do not call! Do something about that issue before launching this listening program.

7. Insofar as is possible, be sure that the same callers go back to call on the same members on the

second round that they called on during the first round.

8. Define a terminal date, usually within four weeks of the beginning day, for each round. The "contract" for that round is completed (a) when the caller has completed five calls or (b) when the time period is up. Do not let this drag out for six months.

9. If some of the callers feel that they absolutely must correct misinformation or respond to a question or tell the people being called upon about a new program, urge them to hold these comments until just before the conclusion of that first visit. If spoken early these comments tend to break the continuity of the listening pattern.

10. It is essential that all callers also are visited by someone. They, too, have something to say! Being called on is a sharply different role than calling and listening. Do not assume the callers will report on "calls" to themselves.

Institutional Maintenance or Innovation?

Perhaps the most common characteristic of any organization as it moves from youth to maturity is to shift the emphasis in the allocation of resources from the creation of the new to the maintenance of the old. This is the eleventh in this list of a dozen common hurdles, pitfalls, and obstacles which the young congregation finds on the road to maturity. In 1973 Westminster Church celebrated its twentieth anniversary. A review of the second ten years of its life revealed several instances where the decision-making processes had moved in the direction of tradition and institutional maintenance rather than toward creativity and innovation.

Perhaps the most serious in terms of the consequences was the decision in the 1960s to construct a new building rather than to build program. A close second was the delay in moving from a "shotgun" to a "rifle" approach in its evangelistic outreach.

The young church tends to use a shotgun approach in evangelism and membership recruitment. One of the reasons this approach usually is reasonably effective is that the young church is very flexible and thus can hear and respond to the different needs of different people. A second reason is that the young church often has a meeting place in the middle of a relatively homogeneous clustering of the population. A third reason is that because of its small size and youth and without a clearly defined pecking order, the young church is usually open to newcomers of all types. A fourth reason is that because of institutional pressures the young church usually exhibits a strong need on its part for additional members. A fifth reason, which may be the most important, is that the young church is still close to that day when the reason for its establishment and continued existence was to reach people with the good news of Jesus Christ and to minister to them. As it becomes older the church may move farther from that original purpose and become trapped by the pressures of institutional maintenance.

By contrast the mature church uses a rifle, not a shotgun, in its evangelistic outreach. The Sunday school for children is a classic example of the use of a more precisely defined group in evangelistic outreach. The Singles Club formed at Westminster in 1972 is an example of this form of selective evangelism. The church with an emphasis on a ministry to "empty nest" couples living in apartments is another. A third is the church with a specialized ministry to young couples with small children of preschool age. A fourth is the church with a specialized ministry to immigrants from Korea. A fifth is the church with a specialized ministry to older, widowed women. One of the distinctions between the young church and the mature church is that the latter has intentionally and systematically developed a more precise approach to its evangelistic outreach than it formerly displayed in an earlier era.

126

Other common examples of this typical tendency to preserve the old, which could be seen at Westminster at the twentieth anniversary celebration, included the desire by many to have only one worship service on Sunday morning; the concern over maintaining the Sunday school at its former level rather than examining other models, both old and new, in Christian education; the concern over maintaining the number, size, strength, and vitality of the women's home Bible study groups rather than to create new groups for new members as these groups were created back in 1960; the tendency (still faintly visible) to focus on maintaining the building rather than to emphasize the use of the building in ministry and service; the obviously greater emphasis on maintaining a favorable financial base rather than to appraise new approaches to the allocation of financial resources; the widespread longing for more home visitation by the new senior minister; the opposition to the plan which had been adopted in 1971 of two different 8:30 worship services on Sunday morning in addition to the traditional 10:30 service; the strong emphasis on perceiving this as a family type congregation even though 63 percent of the adults in the community around the building now live in one-generation households; and the lack of support for the concept of the team ministry inaugurated in 1972 when the third professional staff person was added and the young associate minister left to be replaced by a minister one year older than the senior minister.

The Successor to That First Pastor

The last in this catalog of pitfalls is illustrated by what happened following the departure of the first pastor at Westminster back in 1967. As was mentioned earlier, the first pastor left after fourteen years, expressing the opinion that perhaps a change in ministerial leadership was in order. Four dimensions of this experience at Westminster Church are worth lifting up to illustrate what may happen following the departure of the very able and popular founding pastor of a young and growing congregation.

The most predictable was that the new minister turned out to be an interim or transitional pastor. While he came to what everyone assumed would be a permanent pastorate, he left twenty-two months later. In a substantial majority of churches in which a very popular minister leaves after a fifteen- or twenty-year pastorate, the successor turns out to be the transitional minister between two long-term pastorates.[2]

The second element in this change of pastors is closely related to the first, but far more subtle. The first pastor had helped to train the members to accept him as a very stable "reference point" who knew the entire history of the congregation and knew every member. In effect, he had seniority over every member. By 1965 he was one of the few remaining "pioneers" left at Westminster, and the only pioneer to know every "homesteader" by name. He had been able to meet and get acquainted with every member, one-by-one, as they joined this new congregation. He became the walking bridge between the old and the new. When he left, he had had anywhere between seven and fourteen years to deepen his relationship with the older half of the congregation.

By contrast, his successor arrived one day and found himself the newest of the new homesteaders. He knew nothing of the earlier days of this parish or of the relationships among the members. Instead of becoming acquainted with the members on a one-by-one basis over fourteen years, he had to get acquainted with 933 members—one-half of whom were at least partially inactive—all at once. With the exception of one family who had been members of his

[2] For a more detailed discussion of this subject see Lyle E. Schaller, *The Pastor and the People* (Nashville: Abingdon Press, 1973), pp. 56-64.

former parish, he did not have any deep, long-time, established relationship with any of the 933 members.

With the passage of time the members at Westminster had come to expect "our pastor" to know everyone, to be able to greet them by name, to inquire about a recent event in their lives, or to ask about their family. For many months the new minister was unable to meet this expectation.

The third dimension of this change in ministers turned a difficult task into an impossible one. Even the closest friends of the first pastor were aware that church attendance had declined since the peak back in 1962 and the influx of new members had dropped off sharply. While they sincerely regretted his resignation, many of the members were inclined to agree with the departing minister's comment, "Perhaps a new face in the pulpit and a new voice at board meetings will help produce a new surge of interest among the people here at Westminster." To some extent this expectation was fulfilled. Church attendance did begin to climb and the number of new members joining Westminster did show a sharp increase. This appeared to validate the frequently heard cliche, "A new minister brings in new members and reactivates some of the old members."

What no one had anticipated, however, was that when the Westminster train stopped to let the pastor of fourteen years off and to pick up a new minister, this also was a very convenient stop for several dozen members, including some of the most active leaders, to get off the Westminster train. This group included several families who had joined Westminster back in the earlier days when they had first moved into the neighborhood. Since then a change in the size of the family or an increase in income had motivated them to move to a new residence in another part of the metropolitan area. They continued to drive back to Westminster, partly because that was easier than getting acquainted in a strange church, partly because of friendship ties and "shared roots," [3] and partly because of their attachment to the pastor. When he left, they decided "this was as good a time as any" to transfer to a congregation closer to their place of residence. This group also included several families who had a variety of other reasons for leaving Westminster, but each had postponed the decision because of loyalty to the pastor or because they did not want anyone to believe they were unhappy with the minister.

Thus, during the new minister's first twelve months at Westminster the number of accessions to the membership roll was higher than the two previous years combined, but the number of transfers out more than tripled the number for the previous year. One result was that for the first time in its fifteen-year history Westminster closed a year with fewer names on the membership roster than were there at the beginning of the year.

As the months passed, other areas of discontent, which had received limited discussion in previous years out of deference to the stature of the first pastor, began to be talked about more openly. As this happened it freed people to voice other feelings of dissatisfaction. By the end of eighteen months it was obvious to many that this new minister was not competent to solve all of Westminster's problems. Instead of the problems diminishing in size and number, they seemed to be more numerous and more severe. There clearly was more open discontent throughout the parish. Perhaps another change in ministers was in order? Having had the experience for the first time in the history of this congregation of replacing a pastor, this idea now was much easier to contemplate than it would have been five years earlier. Four months later the second minister had departed for a "new opportunity."

[3] See chapter one, "Commitment and Assimilation."

Hopefully, as members from other congregations founded in the 1950s and the 1960s review these experiences of Westminster Church, they will identify with some of them. Reflecting about what happened at Westminster may help avoid the temptation to look for a scapegoat and may encourage them to analyze their situation in a manner that will produce creative and productive plans for ministry.

7

The Saturday Evening Post Church

Most Americans who today are in the over-forty age bracket have fond memories of the pretelevision era when the weekly arrival of *The Saturday Evening Post* or *Collier's* was an important and eagerly awaited event in millions of homes. The mass-circulation magazine with features designed to appeal to each member of the average family reached its peak in the era between, approximately, 1925 and 1955. *Post, Collier's, Liberty, The American,* and *The Literary Digest* were followed by the mass-circulation picture magazines *Life* and *Look.*

The coming of television communications and advertising killed the general-appeal, mass-circulation magazine. When *Life* suddenly died in December, 1972, an observer of the publishing industry commented, "Well, I guess it was inevitable. Magazines are in trouble all over. Advertisers simply aren't interested in print media."

Church people today can echo, "The same thing is happening in church journalism." *Presbyterian Life,* which once had a huge circulation, has merged with the *United Church Herald* to publish *A.D.* as a joint magazine for the two denominations. The Lutheran Church-Missouri Synod has terminated its general family magazine, *This Day.* The Christian Church (Disciples of Christ) has merged *The Christian* and *World Call* to produce a new periodical, *The Disciple.* The United Methodists terminated their general family magazine, *Together,* which at one time had over a million subscribers, but was down to less than a quarter of that figure at the end. A new periodical, *United*

Methodists Today, replaced both *Together* and *The Christian Advocate.* In the church, as elsewhere, the general-purpose, mass-circulation, broad-appeal magazine has a very limited market today. Does this mean the end of magazine publishing? Hardly. In fact, more magazines are published today than ever before in America's history. What has ended is the era of the mass-circulation magazine which tries to include something for everyone.

This new publishing era is filled with magazines edited for very precisely defined audiences. Even several of the established women's magazines are directed at very specific audiences rather than toward women in general. Dozens of new sports magazines appeal to persons interested only in bowling, or only in tennis, or in professional football, or college football, or archery, or golf, or baseball, or sailing, or stock car racing, or motorcycles. Business magazines are more sharply defined than ever. There are magazines for the owners of specific breeds of pets, for hobbyists, or for owners of private airplanes. *The Reader's Digest* stands alone today as the major exception to this trend which has closed one era and opened another in the publishing industry.

Many Americans over forty have fond memories of the churches they attended in the 1920s, 1930s, and 1940s—churches with their large Sunday school classes, their picnics, and their strong appeal to all ages. They have nostalgic regret over the decline in both the number and size of Sunday school classes. Today church school attendance is only half or perhaps only a fifth of what it was at its peak.

Some of those who look back display a characteristic often attributed to the backward-looking—some of what they remember so fondly and so clearly never actually happened. Still, in many large churches there was a broadly based general appeal to a wide range of people and to the entire family. Often the Sunday school was the entry point for newcomers into the congregation. Many children and adults first joined a Sunday school class and later became members of the congregation. Others joined a Sunday school class, but never united with the congregation. Frequently the attendance at Sunday school exceeded the attendance at worship services.

In the 1948–1963 era many congregations built new educational wings to accommodate the crowds of the pre-1955 era. Some of these new structures were filled for several years following their completion. Other congregations hoped the attraction of a new building would mean a return to the "good old days," but instead saw their Sunday school attendance continue to decline.

As the years have passed, these churches, many of which had been established to serve growing residential neighborhoods of the 1920s or the 1950s, have seen their members scatter over an increasingly large geographical area. Members who had their roots deeply embedded in "the old home church" would travel back to it, sometimes 15 or 25 miles several times a week, for program and administrative responsibilities. Many of these came to fit into that category of congregations described as ex-neighborhood churches in chapter three. During the 1960s a growing number of these older members' children began to assume leadership responsibilities. By the early seventies a substantial number of the leaders, often a majority, have come to be persons who have grown up in the church or are the husbands or wives of members who grew up in its Sunday school. Usually, when this group exceeds thirty percent of the total leadership, that is a sign of a declining church.

What Happened Next?

Today most of these congregations are taking their places in one of these categories:

1. Relocated to a new site on the periphery of the city, frequently only a year or two or three after remodeling the old building at the old location.
2. Merged with another congregation.
3. Dissolved following sale of the property, often as the result of some public-improvement project such as a new highway or urban renewal.
4. Diminished to one-third to one-half of peak strength, but with no major change in the definition of its role.
5. Launched out on a new era with a sharply redefined role as an intentional nongeographical parish to serve a precisely defined new "clientele."
6. Continues to exist as a denominationally assisted "mission" in an effort to "serve the neighborhood."
7. Is living out its days (clearly numbered) as a "chaplaincy" ministry to a diminishing, aging, scattered membership.
8. Shares a minister with another congregation or is served by a part-time minister in an effort to conserve resources and extend its life.
9. Continues a varied but sparsely attended program in a relatively new or recently remodeled building, thanks to the income from a large endowment fund and the support of several second and third generation families.
10. Follows a *Reader's Digest* pattern by investing large quantities of resources in advertising, promotion, and contests to attract a new constituency to the old format at the old location.

The era of the family-oriented, Sunday school church, like the era of the mass-circulation, general-purpose, family-oriented magazine, has come to an end. There are two major exceptions: those few churches which, along with *Life* magazine, limped into the 1970s in the hope that this new decade would bring a return to an old era, and those small-town churches which reach and serve the same people who still are reached and served by *Grit*, the venerable weekly for small-town families that keep going on and on.

What Are the Alternatives?

What is ahead for the family-oriented church which, along with magazines like *Life* and *Together*, flourished during the late 1950s and the early 1960s?

One alternative is to clutch firmly to past glories for as long as possible, even though all the indicators suggest a bleak future.

Another is to try to reconstruct or recapture the past, as the new editors of *The Saturday Evening Post* are doing. According to a recent advertisement, the *Post* is back, now on a monthly schedule "for imaginative folks who remember what life was like before there were riots, tight dollars, and terrible trash."

There is a market for nostalgia, for attempts at recapturing yesterday, for pretending that the changes of the 1960s did not happen. A few magazines—and a great many churches—are attempting to serve people who hope that next year will mark a return to yesterday. As the publishers of the *Post* demonstrate by their less frequent publishing schedule, however, a little nostalgia goes a long way today.

A third alternative is to accept and affirm the fact that a new year brings both new opportunities and new problems, that the black revolution, the youth revolt, women's liberation, and the other changes of the past dozen years are real, that this is a new day in God's world, and that new approaches are necessary to meet the needs of people in an increasingly complex society.

This does not require a repudiation of the role of the church and its programs of the past, but rather an acceptance that in a new day new forms may be needed to bring the gospel of Jesus Christ to people.

These new forms already include new administrative structures in more than a dozen denominations as well as a series of new religious periodicals. Another of the alternatives for this new day can be illustrated by taking a second look at magazine publishing.

What Is Your Specialty?

One of the most interesting segments of the magazine publishing market is monopolized by two periodicals. The market is brides-to-be and their mothers. The publications are *Modern Bride* and *Brides*. In sharp contrast to the old *Saturday Evening Post,* both are aimed at a very narrowly and precisely defined audience. The primary market for these two publications consists of women who are engaged to be married. While the engagement period for the average bride-to-be has doubled since 1960 and now is approximately eleven months, this is still a very highly specialized market. The total number of marriages is now averaging about 2.3 million per year (compared to 1.6 million annually in the 1955–56 era) or an average of approximately 200,000 per month. First-time brides now total 1.8 million annually or an average of 150,000 monthly. Each magazine averages a circulation of approximately 350,000 copies for each of the six issues published annually and the publishers claim that four out of five first time brides will read at least one issue of one of the two periodicals, and one-half of the new brides-to-be in the typical month will read both publications.

During the same years that the *Saturday Evening Post, Collier's, Life, Look,* and other mass-circulation, family-oriented, general publications were folding, these two highly specialized periodicals were thriving. They rank first and third among all consumer magazines in the ads-per-issue category.

What does this say to the "Saturday Evening Post" type of congregation? An obvious answer is to look at the opportunities for specialized ministry to precisely and narrowly defined groups of people. This concept can be illustrated by comments from leaders in several congregations that have gone down this road.

"In addition to our regular program we have identified a ministry to visually handicapped people as our special emphasis for the next several years."

"As a downtown church we have most of the programs and ministries that you would expect to find in a 1200-member congregation in the central business district. In addition, however, we have developed what we call our 'Shadow of the Church' program. This is an intensive effort to respond to the needs of the residents in a three-block by six-block area immediately south of our church building."

"As a small open country church we had to limit our area of specialization to one subject. For us the most logical outreach program was a ministry to the migrant workers who are here for about six or seven weeks every summer."

"Several years ago we decided the top priority for this congregation was to be an agent of reconciliation in a racially divided society. While we carry on a more or less conventional program in such areas as worship, education, nurture, and growth and community service, this is overshadowed by the fact that we are deliberately a biracial congregation. Approximately one-half of our members are white and one-half are black. Being a racially integrated congregation in a racially divided world is our specialty."

"Our people concluded that the day has come when the church cannot be dominated by the clergy. In this larger four-congregation parish we specialize in training laymen for ministry and service, enabling them to be effective ministers. Laymen are responsible for over one-half of the preaching, four-fifths of the pastoral calling, nine-tenths of the counseling, and nearly all the administrative responsibilities in this parish."

"We have a unique location here with the state

prison only two miles away. As a result our major emphasis beyond the traditional ministry to our members and to the community is to the prisoners and to some of the parolees with whom we have built up a continuing relationship."

"Because of the age of our members and the large number of widows, we have developed a specialized ministry to widowed women in the over-fifty age group who have been widowed between six and ten months. We have found that many women at first reject the idea and role of widowhood. After the shock of their husbands' death has worn off and after the friends who flock around them in a supportive role in the weeks following the funeral begin to drift away, we begin to come in, and since everyone in our group is a widow, we can help this newly widowed woman adjust to the new role which has been thrust upon her."

These seven paragraphs illustrate one of the most significant trends in the local church today. This is the growing number of congregations that have selected a field of specialization *in addition* to their traditional ministry to their members and their community.

In some of the larger congregations this may include two or three or four specialized ministries. For example, one Episcopal parish has identified a preventive health care program for the elderly, specialized educational needs of teenagers, a health clinic in poverty community, and support of a community organization as its four areas of specialization.

Smaller congregations usually find it best to concentrate on one area of specialization at a time. Housing programs, community organization efforts, tutor programs, day care centers, biracial vacation church schools, nursery schools, and Christian education programs for handicapped persons are among the more common examples of specialization by congregations in the 75- to 700-member range.

As a parish contemplates identifying and developing its own specialty, it often is helpful to keep in mind these six guidelines.

First, be as precise as possible in identifying the issue of the population group. "A ministry to young people" or "a ministry to the elderly" or "a ministry to the drug scene" or "alcoholism" or "a ministry to the poor" or "unwed mothers" are all meaningless generalizations. Each one must be defined in more limited and precise terms before it provides the "handles" a congregation or a task force must have to begin identifying needs and mobilizing resources.

Second, recognize the distinction between specialized ministries on issues and specialized ministries to people. Rarely is one congregation able to respond effectively to an issue. Issue-centered ministries usually require the cooperation of at least several congregations. By contrast, many ministries to persons can be carried out effectively by one congregation acting unilaterally.

Third, regardless of whether the first choice is an issue- or a person-centered ministry, look around for potential allies! The allies may be other congregations, denominational agencies, secular organizations, public agencies, or individuals. The emphasis is on ministry, not headlines or credit.

Fourth, regardless of the size of the congregation or the type of specialized ministry, there will be some people who will not understand why "our church" should be involved in "that." Expect and plan to go the second and third mile in helping everyone understand what is being undertaken and why. The New Testament is a useful reference book in this effort.

Fifth, early in the process of developing a specialty the persons responsible for recommending the area of specialization should develop a list of at least four different possibilities. It is from this list of possibilities that the area of specialization should be selected. One of the criteria for making the final choice should be the degree of need. Another should be urgency. A third should be the resources and potential capability of the congregation. Not infrequently a congregation gives the highest priority, because of its resources and capabilities, to what is only a second or third priority in terms of need.

Finally, build into the design of the plan for this specialized ministry a basis for subsequent evaluation of the effort. This evaluation may be by some of your own members or by an outside person or agency, but it is important that provision for evaluation be in the original plan.

Now, what is the specialty of your church?

Creativity or Verbal Skills?

The most obvious difference between the current version of the *Saturday Evening Post* and *Highlights* is that while both are monthly publications, the former is aimed at mature adults and the latter is published for children. A less obvious, but more significant difference is that *Highlights* places a premium on the creativity of the reader while the *Post* emphasizes verbal skills.

In most Protestant congregations founded during the past century the early years placed a premium on creativity. The pioneering years at Westminster Church described in chapter six offer one illustration of this emphasis on creativity. Both the demands and the rewards for creativity are very high in the early years of the life of a congregation. Now, before going back to alternatives before the "Saturday Evening Post" type of church, please reflect on these four statements.

1. God is the creator.
2. Man was created in the image of God.
3. Man feels the greatest sense of fulfillment when he is being creative.
4. In a national study of dissatisfaction and alienation among persons in the American labor force, construction workers and the self-employed, as groups,

ranked lowest in dissatisfaction with their jobs. The persons in these two groups reported themselves to be more satisfied with what they were doing than any other group whether the group was defined by race, age, sex, income, collar color, marital status, or occupation.[1]

Does the typical Saturday Evening Post church place the greatest emphasis on verbal skills or on creativity? Which is the emphasis in selecting people for the governing board? Which is emphasized in the pedagogical style of the Sunday school?

A simple test of this concept is the project to remodel, renovate, or repair part of the church building or the parsonage. This is to be carried out with a large proportion of volunteer labor. Are there some men helping in this project who refuse to serve on the governing board, never attend Sunday school, and only rarely participate in the corporate worship service on Sunday morning?

Another test of this concept is to ask the question, How does the reward system in the congregation operate? Are the greatest and most highly visible rewards for creativity or for verbal skills? For doing things with one's hands or for doing things with words?

Or it may be helpful to ask the question, Is competence in verbal skills a distinctive characteristic of the new members who are quickly assimilated into the life and fellowship of the congregation as contrasted with new members who are not so readily assimilated?

When the annual bazaar sponsored by the women's organization was terminated, when the spring pancake supper by the men was discontinued, and when the all-church picnic was dropped, what new avenues for participation emphasizing creative abilities, rather than verbal skills, were adopted to replace these?

[1] Harold L. Sheppard and Neal Q. Herrick, *Where Have All the Robots Gone? Worker Dissatisfaction in the 70s* (New York: Free Press, 1972).

This question concerning verbal skills and creativity leads into another area which may merit examination in the Saturday Evening Post church.

Is There a Future for the Adult Sunday School Class?

"How many adult Sunday school classes are there in your church?"

"We used to have five, but now we only have two," replied a member in her sixties from the Westlawn Church. "Our large adult class is for younger married couples, mostly people past forty, and the one I am in is for older folks, but it's only half the size it used to be."

"We're a six-year-old new mission," responded a layman from Redeemer. "We don't have any adult classes. It takes all of the wives, and the few men who are willing to be involved, to run the Sunday school for the children and youth."

"We still have a fairly strong adult Sunday school here at Central Church," replied a third person who is a member of a congregation which is almost the prototype for the Saturday Evening Post church, "but it's not as large as it used to be. People don't seem to be interested in Sunday school anymore. My wife and I are the newest members of the Couples Class, and we joined seven years ago."

Responses such as these to inquiries about the adult Sunday school are not uncommon. When heard time after time, they tend to reinforce the widely shared impression that the adult Sunday school class will be joining *Collier's*, the ink blotter, the crank-operated telephone, the Philadelphia A's, the convertible, the five-cent package of chewing gum, and the silk stocking as popular elements of American society during the first half of the twentieth century which disappeared during the second half. The comments underscore the relevance of the question, "Is there a future for the adult Sunday school class?"

The future of the adult Sunday school class does not appear very promising if it is viewed as the basic element of the educational ministry for adults. The brief length of the Sunday school hour (often only a forty- or fifty-minute period); the irregular attendance patterns; the time required for reconstituting the group every week, for announcements, and various diversions; the tradition of not expecting any homework by members of the adult class; the inability of so many classes to recruit, receive, and assimilate new members—all these suggest that the congregation which is serious about adult Christian education must look to other alternatives. These include the two- or three-hour special study group one evening a week for six or eight or ten weeks, the transformation of the traditional Men's Bible Class from a Sunday morning lecture to a serious Bible study and/or prayer group meeting at 6 A.M. every Tuesday, the intensive six- or eight- or ten-month training program for all new adult members including intradenominational transfers, the weekend retreat, the once-a-year "University" with several elective courses meeting weekly for a month or two, and the combination mission study-Christian witness visit to the work of the Christian Church on another continent.

On the other hand, it appears there may be a great future for the adult Sunday school class if attention is given to several basic factors which have produced tens of thousands of meaningful adult classes in Protestant churches all across the nation.

These are the classes which the members apparently find to be a very significant part of their lives, which offer the members meaningful opportunities for personal and spiritual growth, which often include a profound interest in the power of prayer, which may emphasize a serious study of the Bible and the role of the Christian Church in contemporary society, and which also may function as very important mutual support groups for the members.

There appears to be a need and a place for these adult Sunday school classes in many congregations, regardless of the denominational label on the meeting place or the socioeconomic class of the members or the place on the theological spectrum of the congregation.

The place, role, and future of the adult Sunday school has been strengthened by (1) the growing recognition of the importance of small groups in congregations with several hundred members, (2) the renewed emphasis on serious Bible study, and (3) the contemporary swing toward a more personal religious emphasis.

After studying the role, life, vigor, strengths, and weaknesses of many adult classes, it appears those with the bright futures possess most, and occasionally all, of these ten common characteristics in addition to those mentioned earlier.

1. The class is more than a class, it is a cohesive group. The members feel and express a loyalty to that group. For many members this class is where they first met many of the people who today are their closest personal friends.

2. The class meets together for some form of social event at least eight or ten times a year. Frequently the attendance for these social events exceeds the attendance on Sunday morning (partly because some of the members of the class are serving as teachers of other classes on Sunday morning). These social events often appear to be the "glue" that holds the class together. In many classes the Sunday attendance is highest on the Sunday immediately following a monthly social event.

An important dimension of the social life of the class is when the members eat together several times a year. This may be the monthly social event; it may be an occasional "covered dish" or "carry in" dinner; it may be picnics and other outings; it may be only coffee and rolls every Sunday before the class convenes. Not infrequently it is a combination of several of these.

3. The class has a series of common tasks, each of which serves as a focal point for group effort. At one time it may be a special study venture requiring homework by every member, at another time it may be an outreach or mission project or a special effort to aid the church of which the class is a part.

4. The class has its own treasury and receives an offering from the members every week which goes into the class treasury to finance class projects. While the existence of these numerous treasuries may disturb some church leaders (including some ministers) who believe there should be only one treasurer for the entire congregation, most strong adult classes with a long history do have their own treasury and finance their own special projects.

5. The class has one or more yearly goals which are quantified and progress in reaching the goal(s) is reported to the members regularly and clearly.

The goal may be to raise a specific amount of money for missions or to receive a certain number of new members or to make a specified number of visitation-evangelism calls or to remodel a room in the church building or to pave the parking lot or to "sponsor" a specialized ministry or to finance the cost of a special event for the church's youth or to visit the sick and the shut-ins or some other venture. Regardless of the content of the goal, it is specific, achievable, measurable, and visible.

6. One of the most important significant characteristics of the strong adult Sunday school class is a deliberate effort to identify and respond to several different religious needs of the members. These may include Bible study, theological discussions, and current issues.

7. The class meets in "its own place." It does *not* move from place to place, but has an assigned meeting place and everyone, especially persons not mem-

bers of that class, feel that the class "owns" that meeting place. A shift to another meeting place on a temporary basis for a few weeks often results in a decrease in attendance. This often is overlooked by many younger church leaders who fail to recognize that for many older adults their primary identification with the congregation is with this class. When the meeting place is moved, it threatens this point of primary identification because it seems to diminish the status, role, and importance of the class.

8. The least common of the characteristics on this list is the ability of the adult Sunday school class to identify, recruit, receive, and assimilate new members. The best of the contemporary adult classes, however, do work at this intentionally and systematically and/or encourage and facilitate the formation of new classes for new adult members of the congregation and for older members who never became a part of one of the existing classes.

9. Another characteristic of the best adult Sunday school classes, and this also is far from universal, is a continuing effort to support and undergird the total ministry and program of both the congregation and the denomination. This is not necessarily a completely uncritical support, but it reflects a positive attitude rather than the "separatist" feeling or the isolationism which has characterized many adult Sunday school classes in the past. This supportive and cooperative attitude of the best of the contemporary adult classes is winning them the strong support of some of the pastors who formerly viewed the large, strong adult class as a rival or a threat.

10. Finally, and perhaps most significant of all, the members of these adult classes enjoy being with one another. To some degree every Sunday morning is "homecoming," and there is a sense of joy at being together again. Many of the members arrive ten or twenty or thirty minutes early and frequently the class finds it very difficult to adjourn on time.

HEY, THAT'S OUR CHURCH!

Yes, there appears to be a future for those adult Sunday school classes which display the characteristics described here. The use of this check list may be helpful in the self-evaluation process of the adult Sunday school. It could be a means of helping the Saturday Evening Post type of congregation move into a new era in its history.

8
Characteristics of the Contemporary Church

If the Saturday Evening Post type of church is representative of yesterday, what are the characteristics of the emerging church of the 1970s and 1980s?

There are many signs that suggest a new religious revival is beginning to occur on the North American continent. There are many signs that suggest the religious activism of the 1960s has been replaced by a new religious pietism for the 1970s. There are many signs that suggest young adults and youth have a different set of expectations of the church in the 1970s than their counterparts expressed in the 1960s.

The expectations of people for the church do change from decade to decade, and these expectations do influence the definition of the purpose and role of the parish in the contemporary world. As we look at the 1970s and look ahead to the 1980s, what are the characteristics of the contemporary church for this era? Based on this observer's travels, on conversations with others, and on what has been written on the subject, it is clear that a new type of church is emerging. The contemporary church is still one of the rarer types of parishes on the ecclesiastical scene today. It is a church that is living and serving in the midst of contemporary reality, a place where many people like to visit, but few want to live.

From visits to what appear to be representative congregations of this emerging new type of church it is possible to suggest a checklist which reflects some of the important characteristics of the contemporary church.

1. Perhaps the most distinctive characteristic of the contemporary church is that the leaders have identified a New Testament definition of the purpose and role of the worshiping congregation in the world and are seeking to have their congregation be faithful to that definition and obedient to the call of the Lord today in this place. The contemporary church has achieved a high degree of self-identity. It knows who it is and the members reflect this. This is the foundation for intentionality.

2. From another perspective the contemporary church is perceived by both insiders and outsiders as a supportive, affirmative, and redemptive fellowship. The visibility of this characteristic is reflected, not so much by words and slogans, but rather by the program of the congregation and the actions of individual members. The performance exceeds the rhetoric.

3. Closely related to this characteristic is a very strong emphasis on enhancing the quality of the Christian life for each individual. In programatic terms this includes study groups for spiritual and personal growth, a variety of opportunities for people to be *directly* involved in ministry, a pluralistic approach to corporate worship, cross-generational classes at least occasionally in the church school, representatives from all generations in the membership in the policy making and governing bodies of the congregation, greater lay participation in worship, an obvious sense of intentionality in increasing the choices available to people, and a pluralistic approach to education, nurture, and fellowship opportunities for members.

4. Consistent with these other characteristics is the healthy group life of the contemporary church. There is an affirmative effort to function, not simply as a congregation of individuals and families, but also as a congregation of groups. It is easy for the outsider and

the insider to identify the many groups within the congregation in which membership in *that* group is especially meaningful to a substantial number of persons in the group. These groups range from the choir to Sunday school classes (especially some adult classes) to growth groups to committees to service-oriented groups to the women's organization to a variety of short-term groups organized to meet the special needs of people to classes for new members to a men's prayer breakfast group. Three simple tests of the health of the group life are (1) ask how many groups there are in which the membership in that group is especially meaningful to the members, (2) ask what proportion of the total membership is actively involved in groups which they find to be meaningful, and (3) ask *after* a meeting of any group, organization, committee, class, etc., "How many of those present were glad they were here?" (Sometimes the answer to this question can be seen in how quickly or how slowly people leave after the adjournment time.)

5. One of the decisive characteristics of the contemporary church that distinguishes it from many other congregations is that its orientation is toward today and tomorrow, not toward doing yesterday over again. The contemporary church carries only a modest weight of baggage labeled "precedent" or "custom" or "tradition."

6. Another decisive characteristic of the contemporary church is the growing emphasis on a shared style of leadership, including both ordained and lay leaders in all aspects of the decision-making process. The pastor is not *the* leader, but rather is one of the leaders. This is not to suggest that a completely nondirective style of pastoral leadership is a hallmark of the contemporary church. It isn't! That is a characteristic of some congregations of the 1950–1965 era, but not of the 1970s. In the 1970s leaders do lead, but it is shared leadership. The leaders suggest, advise,

counsel, initiate, cause things to happen, and manage situations, not people. The pastor is both able and willing to work hard to launch a new ministry and is able to turn it over completely to lay leaders once it is launched.

This style of shared leadership means that lay persons are assumed to have an active rather than a passive role in all dimensions of the life and ministry of the parish.

7. Closely related to this is broad ownership of the goals of the parish. A test is to ask, "Are the persons responsible for implementing the goals in ministry, service, outreach, program, and housekeeping responsibilities also involved in formulating these goals?"

8. Another distinctive characteristic of the contemporary church is that the members do not anticipate that the youth in today's congregation will be the leaders of that same congregation twenty or thirty years hence.

For many people, including some in nearly every congregation, this is a most difficult concept to accept. They see today's youth as the nucleus for tomorrow's church, and frequently this is the most common stated reason for placing a major emphasis on a youth ministry. One of the easiest means of testing the validity of this assumption is either (a) review the names of the persons in the youth fellowship of 1955 or the members of the high school membership class of the early 1960s and determine how many are members of this congregation today and /or (b) list the names of today's leaders and discover how many of these persons were members of *this* congregation back when in their teens.

When the second of these two procedures is followed, the results in *urban* parishes usually reveals one of two conditions. Either the proportion of the present leaders who were reared in that congregation is under thirty percent *or* the congregation is experiencing a decline in the total number of members.

9. Closely related to this is the willingness and the *capability* of the contemporary church to accept and assimilate new people into the life and fellowship of the congregation. One beginning point is to ask such questions as these and compare the answers: How many adults joined this congregation during the past twenty-four months? When did the newest member of the congregation on the governing board join this congregation? How old is the youngest couple in the young married couples Sunday school class? How many adults in leadership positions joined this congregation during the past three years? How far back do you have to go to find that date since one-half of the confirmed members united with *this* congregation?

10. One of the most distinctive characteristics of the contemporary church can be discovered by asking individuals who have joined the congregation recently, "In looking back on your life, why are you a member of *this* parish, rather than some other congregation here in this community?"

In the traditional church many people answer with such responses as, "My parents were members here." or "My spouse was a member here before we were married so naturally, after we were married, I transferred my membership to this congregation." or "The pastor called on us soon after we moved into our present home, and I guess that's why we're members here." or "When we moved here this was the closest church of our denomination."

In the contemporary church more people respond with such answers as, "When we moved here we shopped five churches and picked this as the one that met our needs." or "I happened to visit here with a friend one Sunday, and when I saw a congregation that includes many grey heads, several blacks of all ages, lots of young adults, and quite a few couples with children, I decided somebody must be doing something right, and so I transferred my membership here." or "We're members here because of what this church is doing in ministry and outreach to nonmembers." or "This is the first church I've ever been in where I found the worship service to be a really meaningful experience."

11. An essential characteristic of the contemporary church of the 1970s is a willingness to change structures, schedules, customs, and organizations in order to accommodate people more adequately rather than to try to change people to fit into the tradition of "but this is the way we've always done it here at St. Paul's."

This is one of the major distinctions between the contemporary church and the traditional one which expects people, be they newcomers to the community, visitors, or children of members, to fit into the pattern of how it "has always been done here." One of the lessons of the 1960s was that the congregation which is able and willing to change its institutional patterns to accommodate people tends to be more effective in reaching people than the church which expects people to change to fit *this* congregation's "way of doing things."

12. Another hallmark of the contemporary church is that the emphasis on creativity exceeds the emphasis on verbal skills.[1]

13. One of the major differences between the contemporary church and the church of the 1960s is the sense of affirmative expectations that are widely shared by members of the contemporary church. This is in part a reflection of the emphasis on creativity and stands in sharp contrast to the gloomy expectations that were a characteristic of many churches in the 1960s.

14. Closely related to this is the feeling of genuine joy expressed by many members of the contemporary church. This joyous feeling may be expressed and felt

[1]See chapter seven, "Creativity or Verbal Skills," for a more extended discussion of this point.

during corporate worship, in what in other congregations are often dreary business meetings, in the church school, in the tone of voice of members as they greet one another as well as in the expectations about what the future holds.

One of the reasons for this pervasive sense of joy is that an intentional effort has been made to make being a member of this congregation an enjoyable experience. Instead of exploiting volunteers and discarding them when they are exhausted by a combination of overwork and frustrations, the contemporary church consciously cares for the volunteer and his spiritual and psychological health.

This means the role of the individual has to be meaningful to him personally and spiritually. This means that for most members being a member of the contemporary church should be a growth experience. This means that the "rewards" of frustration, disappointment, and disillusionment must be heavily overbalanced by the psychic satisfactions of being a faithful and obedient servant of God, by a sense that one is part of an organization which is communicating the Gospel of Jesus Christ through both word and deed, and by the knowledge that "my church" knows where it is going and is making commendable progress in reaching identifiable goals.

Another reason behind this sense of joy is the emphasis on creativity. Creativity produces a sense of fulfillment which often is expressed as joy.

15. One of the easiest characteristics of the contemporary church to identify and measure is that women are treated as children of God and as fully equal to men. In some denominations, such as Episcopal, Lutheran, Disciples of Christ, and Presbyterian, this change is still being opposed in many parishes by substantial numbers of men and some women.

16. One of the most difficult to define characteristics of the contemporary church is its role on community issues. The contemporary church takes very

seriously *both* of the great commandments of Jesus. How this is translated into operational terms varies tremendously from place to place and parish to parish. One of the few consistent threads is that the contemporary church increasingly is concerned with changing the structures, institutions, and systems of society on a long-term basis rather than with narrowly defined and specific questions such as candidates for office, legislative questions, or issues in a referendum. For example, instead of supporting or opposing specific individuals for positions on the board of education, the contemporary church might be dealing with the question of whether or not there should be alternatives for every person entering first grade.

The contemporary church also recognizes the need for alliances if a ministry is to be enhanced and effective, and therefore it is both able and willing to enter into cooperative arrangements with other Christian congregations.

17. Closely related to this is the recognition by the contemporary church that it is not living in a hospitable culture or community. This is one of the distinctive differences between the contemporary church and the Saturday Evening Post church which saw itself, often accurately, as existing in a community which was compatible with and supportive of the traditions, values, and life style of that type of church.

18. Closely related to both of the previous points is the definition of an active church worker. In the traditional church an active church worker is the person who teaches Sunday school or is chairman of the trustees or serves on four or five parish committees or who is seen frequently around the church building.

In the contemporary church the operational definition of this concept includes the member who has been "promoted" from membership on the church council to membership on the city council, the member who lives the Christian ethic in his daily work, the member who visits the lonely elderly persons in the county nursing home nine miles away, and the high school social studies teacher who carries a heavy burden as an unpaid counselor to the alienated street kids.

19. The contemporary church sees itself as an *inter*dependent element of the universal Christian Church *and practices this concept,* rather than seeing itself as a separate, autonomous, and independent unit in its own cocoon.

The clearest measure of this characteristic is seen in its relationships with *both* the other churches in the community *and* other churches around the world.

This again is in sharp contrast to the pattern which began to emerge in the 1960s when many congregations in the United States reduced their ties and concerns with the churches on other continents in order to "take care of first things first."

20. As suggested earlier, in the contemporary church there is an affirmative attitude toward pluralism and diversity. People are able to accept the fact that what may be meaningful to one person may not be meaningful to everyone.

Thus, while the contemporary church recognizes there are some "givens" for any group of people who identify themselves as a Christian church, the beginning point in relating to other people is the other person's agenda. This can be seen in ministries to nonmembers in the community, in the evangelistic outreach of the church, in its response to visitors and prospective new members, and in defining the form of its ministry in the community.

This remarkable openness to the needs of others and the ability to accommodate an unusual degree of diversity in both the membership and the program appears to be a product of the strong sense of self-identity and intentionality mentioned earlier.

21. The contemporary church recognizes the importance of providing meaningful growth experiences for people. The contemporary church is more likely to

offer a marriage enrichment workshop for members than just a sermon on marriage. The contemporary church is more likely to enable a dozen members to visit the work of the Christian church in another country and have these people share their experiences on many different occasions than to have a special "missions night" one evening every year featuring a missionary on furlough as the speaker. The contemporary church usually provides opportunities for lay persons to read the Scripture lesson on Sunday morning rather than listen to a clergyman read it. The contemporary church is more likely to have a festival of arts than to have a few religious paintings on the walls. All of this is based on the assumption of an active rather than a passive role for the laity, including people outside the membership of that congregation.

22. The contemporary church evaluates its ministry using qualitative as well as quantitative yardsticks. In the contemporary church the leaders are as much interested in the quality of what happened during a specific program or event as they are in the number of people who were present.

23. The leaders in the contemporary church usually choose to ask "Why?" rather than "Who?" when something goes wrong. The emphasis is on analysis and diagnosis rather than on placing the blame and scapegoating.

24. The contemporary Christian church teaches, preaches, and practices an orthodox doctrine of the Trinity. Unlike some churches which appear to have developed an operational definition of the Trinity as consisting of God, Jesus, and the Bible, the contemporary church teaches the Bible as a means to an end. Unlike some other churches today, the contemporary church does not feel threatened by the Holy Spirit. The contemporary church believes with Paul that there are gifts of the Spirit, that spirituality is not one uniform experience, that manifestations of the Spirit can be seen in a wide range of conduct and actions,

and that, by definition, true spirituality cannot be a divisive element in the life of the worshiping congregation.

Now, how many congregations can you name that meet all twenty-four of these criteria? I have yet to find even one that includes this entire list among its distinctive characteristics, but every year I see an increasing number with sixteen, eighteen, twenty, or even twenty-one of these two dozen characteristics present!

9
Survival or Identity?

About thirty miles east of a large urban center is a small but growing city which has a strong attraction for people who seek the benefits of life in a small city, but want urban employment opportunities and are willing to pay the price of commuting fifty to seventy miles daily in order to have both advantages. For the past fifteen years the population increase has been at the rate of 3 to 5 percent per year.

Two blocks north of the heart of the central business district is the meeting place for First Church. Founded approximately eighty-five years ago, this congregation moved into its first permanent meeting place in 1896. A larger building was constructed in 1919. When this burned in 1948, a larger brick church was built and an educational wing was completed in 1964.

As happened with thousands of other congregations all across the nation, the decade following the close of World War II brought dozens of young married couples into First Church. Today many of these people remain as a part of the loyal core of the congregation, although each one is approximately one generation older than he or she was back in the 1950s.

First Church peaked in size and institutional strength back in the late 1950s when the membership figure passed the 800 mark, the combined attendance for the two Sunday morning worship services averaged 425, and the dollar receipts from the membership, including the building fund, totaled $87,800.

Fifteen years later, despite the continued population increase of the city, First Church had dropped in size to 500 resident confirmed members, the worship attendance was down to 195 and the budget had leveled off at $59,000.

During the intervening years the indebtedness on the new educational wing was paid off, morale declined, a new parsonage was acquired, the proportion of inactive members increased, and there were five unhappy and two acceptable experiences with a series of seminary students who served as part-time youth ministers. One of the two acceptable students remained at First Church for two years following his graduation from seminary and served on a full-time basis as a combination youth minister-assistant pastor. During his tenure the youth group peaked in size with eighty to a hundred high school age young people actively related to the church.

Today the high school youth group includes six girls and one boy, and there is a widespread demand that, "We must get a full-time youth minister who can build that program back up to what it used to be. After all, the future of the church rests on the youth. If we don't reach them now, we may miss them forever."

The present pastor, who is in his second year at First Church, is a personable thirty-two-year-old in his second pastorate. He was chosen after the first six choices of the pulpit committee had each rejected the overtures from First Church. He was called in part because it was hoped "a young couple will attract other young couples and everybody knows that we no longer have very many people under forty here at First Church." A second factor in choosing him was that he was willing to come for a salary that turned out to be one hundred dollars below the average beginning salary for all seminary graduates in the denomination that year. A third factor was that he was attracted by the challenge of reversing the downward trend at an old downtown church. He is approximately one full generation younger than the leadership core, most of whom were born before 1925 and have clear firsthand recollections of the impact of the Great Depression.

There is a long series of amber "caution" and red "danger" lights flashing at First Church.

Perhaps the most obvious of these signals is the expectation that the professional staff can and should solve all problems.

The second is the very narrow base of financial support. Twenty percent of the members contribute 75 percent of the dollar receipts and, even worse, 5 percent contributed 51 percent of last year's total receipts!

A third warning signal is that during the period when the community experienced a 60 percent increase in population, this congregation experienced more than a 50 percent decline in worship attendance.

A fourth warning sign is the very heavy emphasis on developing a strong youth program and on calling a full-time youth minister to replace the part-time youth minister when he leaves next summer. This appears to be an emphasis on "salvation of the next generation" rather than on ministry today.

A fifth signal is the vague but easily detectable feeling of "We're not O.K." or "There's something wrong here." This is widespread among most longtime members of congregations which a decade or two ago had a much larger group than today. Because this feeling is widespread, however, does not mean it is good!

Closely related to this is the excessively large number of "blinking red lights." Each one of these represents an unhappy, an unheard, a neglected, a hurt, a frustrated, or an alienated member. At First Church the number of "blinking red lights" appears to be larger than normal. It may be that some of the lights have been blinking for so long the bulb has burned out, and that is why the number of nonparticipating members is so large.

Perhaps the most subtle of these danger signals is the shift toward a "landlord" role. As several members emphasized, this is indeed a "busy building." The day care center, the language classes for Spanish-speaking persons, and the several antipoverty programs housed in the building are all ventures of great merit. They are not, however, ministries of and by this congregation! They are service projects operated by other organizations and involve very few members of this congregation. First Church's role is that of a benevolent landlord. In broad, general terms the historical record suggests that when a congregation shifts from a servant or ministry role to a landlord role this tends to have a very negative impact on the morale, on the evangelistic outreach, on the breadth of the program, and on the congregational care ministry of the landlord congregation.

Another in this series of warning signals at First Church, perhaps, is related to the "blinking red light" issue. At First Church the importance of providing psychic rewards or satisfactions for the volunteers appears to need attention. The old phrase "Feed my sheep" is still relevant. There are many kinds of "food" for volunteers in the church. These include outstanding music, great preaching, meaningful participation in the life of a church with a clearly defined purpose and direction, pastoral care in crisis situations, a pat on the back, pastoral calling, the occasional event at the church which stirs the souls of all present, and participation in meaningful ministries. Some of the volunteers at First Church do not appear to be well fed by such experiences. They cannot be fed vicariously.

Finally, the congregation is organized in a manner which emphasizes participation and representation. Another way of stating this is that First Church has many, many places in the organizational structure where an action proposal can be vetoed, but it lacks a clearly defined process for the introduction, discussion, review, approval, and implementation of new ideas.

What is the basic issue at First Church?

————•————

The Ridgetop Church was founded in 1888 to serve a farming community. Located in the open country, the original building was destroyed by a tornado in 1919 and was replaced by a white frame structure located between the highway and the cemetery. For most of the first sixty years of its life Ridgetop was served by a full-time minister, but the last full-time pastor left in 1948, just after the new parsonage was completed. That new parsonage has proved to be a significant asset, however, and it has been a major factor in the ability of this congregation to attract a series of very competent married students from the theological seminary seventy miles to the south. These students have served as part-time pastors while completing their formal education. Each one usually stays two or three years.

The worship attendance at Ridgetop has ranged between 60 and 80 for decades, and the average for last year was 73. Most of the adult members are (1) farmers, retired farmers, and their wives or widows in the over-sixty age range, (2) couples in the 25-40 age bracket who are farming as single operations what were six or eight separate farms back in the 1930s, and (3) ex-farmers who live in one of the old farmhouses and drive into the city twenty miles to the north to work. There are three families in the congregation who are not related to any other members and who live in new houses that recently were constructed nearby. In two of the families both the husband and wife are employed in the city while the third is a semiretired couple.

During the past five years more than three hundred new homes have been constructed on farms which have been subdivided within two miles of the Ridgetop building. Another seven hundred are proposed for the next five years. What is the basic issue at Ridgetop Church?

———•———

The history of St. Paul's Lutheran Church goes back to 1948 when it was launched as a new mission. A quarter of a century later, after encountering many of the pitfalls described in chapter six, St. Paul's had grown to be a mature congregation with over 2,800 baptized members of whom nearly 2,200 were confirmed members. Worship attendance for the three Sunday morning services has fluctuated between 900 and 1,100 for several years and now averages 910.

The turnover in the membership of this relatively young and very large congregation can be expressed in different ways. At the end of 1973 only one-half of the members of 1955 were still on the membership roll at St. Paul's, but they constituted only 12 percent of the total membership in 1973. One-half of the current members had joined since mid-1967.

The aging of the membership can be seen in the decline in the size of the Sunday school and in the ratio of confirmed to baptized members. During the 1950s approximately 60 percent of the total baptized membership were confirmed members, but by 1973 this figure had climbed to 82 percent. In 1965 it was still below the average for The American Lutheran Church, the parent denomination, of 67 percent. During the next eight years that figure climbed to 72 percent for the denomination, but at St. Paul's it jumped from 59 percent in 1960 to 65 percent in 1965 to 75 percent in 1970 to 81 percent in 1973!

The growth in size and the aging of St. Paul's was accompanied by an increase in the proportion of inactive members. In The American Lutheran Church as a whole, approximately 75 percent of the confirmed members commune at least once a year. At St. Paul's this figure dropped from 85 percent in 1964 to 80 percent in 1968 to 73 percent in 1972.

Another way to describe what was happening at St. Paul's is to view this parish as moving from an era of youth and growth to an era of maturity. Organizationally this change has profound implications for planning for the future. This change can be symbolized by a diagram.

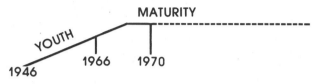

During that first twenty-year period of youth and growth the congregation gathers and assimilates the pioneers around the combination of a Lutheran heritage and exciting contemporary goals. The congregation is relatively homogeneous. The emphasis is on growth. The self-evaluation process is oriented to quantitative indicators. Growth and "progress" are highly visible. There are many satisfactions or psychic rewards for the members in general and for the leaders in particular. The life and decision-making processes of the parish have a strong goal orientation. There is both the need and a variety of opportunities for people to express their gifts of creativity through the church. The commitment of the members to *this parish* is largely focused around contemporary goals rather than a congregational heritage.[1] As the years pass, however, and what was once a new mission becomes a mature parish, the contemporary goals of the 1950s and 1960s become "heritage" in the 1970s. Among other implications, this means it becomes more difficult to receive and assimilate newcomers. The membership goes down and the proportion of inactive members begins to increase.

[1] See chapter one, "Commitment and Assimilation," for an elaboration of this concept.

As what once was a new mission moves into the era of maturity, changes begin to appear. At St. Paul's, as in nearly every other new mission, this can be seen in the net growth by persons joining by letter of transfer from another parish. What was once a large plus figure turns into a minus as the pioneers move on faster than the homesteaders arrive. As the congregation ages, the death rate goes up—from an average of 5.5 deaths per year in 1969 and 1970 to 8.0 per year in 1971-73. The number of baptisms drops from an average of 64 per year in 1969–1970 to 49 per year in 1971–73. The average attendance at Sunday morning worship drops from a peak of nearly 1,100 back in 1968 to slightly over 900 in 1973. As the pioneers move away, the homesteaders moving in attend less frequently than did the pioneers. The total number of annual accessions to the membership roll drops below the number of losses and the total baptized membership drops from 3,051 at the end of 1969 to 2,854 at the end of 1973.

What is the basic issue at St. Paul's?

Transfers

Year	In	Out	Net
1969	167	125	42
1970	152	118	34
1971	117	141	-24
1972	96	102	- 6
1973	122	131	- 9

In 1965 First Evangelical United Brethren (EUB) Church was a thriving congregation of 455 members in a predominantly Protestant midwestern city of 26,000 residents. It was the only EUB church in the city. Every year for more than a decade the pastor had reported a net increase in the membership figure, in the average attendance at worship which topped the 300 mark in 1965 for the first time in the history of the congregation, in the dollar receipts, and in the giving for benevolence. One of the reasons for this consistent growth pattern was the rural-to-urban migration which brought several hundred newcomers to town every year and largely offset the outmigration of persons in the 18-25 age bracket. Some of these newcomers were people who had grown up in one of the rural EUB churches in the surrounding counties. One of the reasons they came to First EUB Church when they moved to town was because most of them knew of the church and many of them had a firsthand acquaintance with the pastor and/or some of the members. First was the largest and strongest EUB congregation in a seven-county region. It was a leadership church with an important role in denominational affairs.

The 1968 merger of the Evangelical United Brethren Church with the Methodist Church resulted in two congregations in this city carrying the name "The First United Methodist Church." Since the former EUB congregation was both smaller and newer than the former First Methodist Church, it was decided that it should be the one to change its name. Faith United Methodist Church was chosen as the new name.

At the end of 1974 Faith United Methodist Church reported a total of 385 members, an average attendance at Sunday morning worship of 210, a decrease for the fourth consecutive year in the dollar receipts, and another drop in both the enrollment and the average attendance in the church school.

What had happened between 1965 and 1973?

This congregation changed from being the leadership church for the denomination in the region to being the third largest, and least well known, of the six United Methodist congregations in this city. Instead of being *the* logical choice for anyone moving to the city from within the EUB family, it became one of six alternatives. It was generally viewed as the second or third most theologically conservative of six United Methodist congregations, so it did not have a clearly defined and distinctive place in those terms. When members from Faith went to a district or conference meeting of the new denomination, they felt like intruders or a minority caucus rather than acknowledged leaders. In 1970 the forty-seven-year-old pastor, who had been serving this congregation since 1900, decided to leave the professional ministry and sell real estate. His successor was a thirty-one-year-old minister who had been reared in a Methodist parsonage by a preacher father who also had been reared in a Methodist parsonage. While the new minister was a very likeable individual, he was perceived as a "liberal" by most of the leaders at Faith, who also were a generation older. By this time Faith was showing more and more signs of being a "heritage" type congregation (see chapter one), but the new minister was largely unacquainted with the EUB heritage in general or that of this congregation in particular. He did carry with him, however, a large quantity of Methodist heritage! So it took him nearly a year to stop saying "Methodist" and learn to say "United Methodist." When the congregation celebrated its ninetieth anniversary on a Sunday afternoon in 1972, the big event of the day was a forty-minute narration of its history from the earliest days. A variety of skits and songs were used to dramatize the narrative. While this was taking place near the front of the stage in the fellowship hall, an artist was drawing pictures on a large white cardboard backdrop at the rear of the stage. When the narrative came to the merger of the Evangelical Church and the United Brethren in 1946, she quickly sketched in a handshake with one hand labeled "Ev." and the other "U.B." When the narrator reached the 1968 merger of the EUB Church with the Methodists, she drew a picture of a tiny fish swimming into the mouth of a very large fish. The only laughter in the room came from the pastor and one new couple who had both been reared in former Methodist congregations.

What is the basic issue at Faith Church?

———•———

The Glenwood Presbyterian Church was established as a new mission in 1949. The site purchased by the presbytery for the meeting place of the new congregation was on the top of a hill near the center of what turned out to be an upper to middle class suburban community.

When the second pastor arrived in 1954, he found a congregation of nearly two hundred families, nearly all of them with two or three school-age children. A strong supporter of the Youth Club approach to weekday Christian education, he inaugurated this program at Glenwood. For three ten-week periods a year for the next two decades Glenwood Presbyterian Church specialized in this one-day-a-week after-school program. From 3:45 P.M. until 8:00 P.M. thirty Wednesdays a year there would be literally hundreds of children at the church for this one-day-a-week program which included formal classes, choir practice, crafts, recreation, discovery groups, confirmation class, and a variety of other activities, including a meal. At its peak in 1964 the attendance averaged 460 young people in addition to the fifty adult volunteers and the three professional staff members. Nearly every family had at least one child go through the Youth Club and many had three or four or five.

By almost any measuring stick it was a tremendous program. It was widely accepted that the Youth Club was the basic reason for the rapid growth in membership at Glenwood and for the ability of this congregation to reach and quickly assimilate newcomers in a community with a high residential turnover.

By 1974 the community was beginning to show its

age. Most of the houses were at least twenty years old. The enrollment in the public schools for the 1974–75 school year was exactly one-half what it had been in 1964–65. One reason for this was the aging of the residents. More than two-thirds of the households on the membership roster at Glenwood Presbyterian Church were one-generation households and the number of one-person households was increasing every year. The second factor in the decline in the public school enrollment and in the size of the Youth Club at the church was the combination of the opening of a large new parochial school by St. Mary's Roman Catholic Church in 1968 and the fact that approximately 80 percent of the new residents were Roman Catholic families. In part this was due to the attraction of St. Mary's, and in part it reflected the exodus from the central city which was following the typical Jewish, white Protestant, white Catholic, and black Protestant sequence.

Individual interviews with fifty leaders at Glenwood Presbyterian Church in mid-1974 included this question, "What is the event or the occasion that you remember most vividly in terms of its meaning for you personally and your relationship to Glenwood Presbyterian Church? Is there a moment, an hour, a day, an event, or a relationship that you have had with, or through, or because of this church which is especially meaningful to you?"

Out of the fifty persons interviewed, thirteen were unable to name any such event, occasion, or relationship. One mentioned seeing a group of young people whom she had taught in the third grade Sunday school class unite with the church several years later. One mentioned the wedding of his youngest daughter. Another referred to a weekend retreat. Two described summer trips they had taken as counselors with the high school youth group. Three responded with the ministry of this church to them during a time of family tragedy. Two said they had first met Christ at

Glenwood Presbyterian Church. One mentioned a specific Bible study group. One referred back to his own wedding in the church. One described a men's early morning prayer group. Twenty-four referred either in general or specific terms to their service as volunteers in the Wednesday Youth Club program. Only three of the thirty-seven described an event or occasion or relationship that had occurred within the past six years.

What is the basic issue at Glenwood Church?

———•———

What do these five congregations have in common? What is the common thread running through these five brief word pictures? What is the basic issue in each congregation?

Each of these five congregations is faced with the need to redefine its identity. Each needs to establish a new role for itself as it turns from the past and begins to plan for the future. Each one has to redefine its identity and to define a new role for itself before goals can be formulated.

In one of the most influential books to be published in the past dozen years, William Glasser made three statements which have a remarkable degree of relevance for some types of churches. "I found that people needed involvement as a prerequisite to change .... Involvement (is) also a prerequisite to a successful role or identity. ... The change from a survival or goal society to an identity or role society is here. ... The institutions of our society still operate as if goal took precedence over role." [2]

These comments appear to offer a useful frame of reference for looking at the questions and issues before these five congregations. In each congregation an era recently ended in which the role or identity of that congregation was reasonably clear. The self-image or identity of the congregation was reinforced

[2] *The Identity Society* (New York: Harper & Row, 1972), pp. 9-10.

by both the general context and the image held by nonmembers. In each case that era has ended and the new role for a new era has yet to be defined.

At First Church the question is, Should this be a middle-sized congregation or should it seek to grow back to at least its former size? Should First Church focus in on ministry to the members—a very tempting alternative? Or should it place a far greater emphasis on an evangelistic outreach? Or should it continue down the path of becoming a passive "landlord" type of operation? What is the new role of First Church? These questions are obscured by the nostalgic longing to recreate the large youth fellowship of yesterday.

The Ridgetop Church is confronted with the choice of attempting to perpetuate yesterday's role as a rural farming community congregation or to redefine a new role as an exurban church.

St. Paul's Lutheran Church has moved from the era of a youthful and growing new mission into the stage of being a mature, very large, and increasingly complex parish. This is raising a long series of difficult questions.

Faith Church lost its identity as a result of the EUB-Methodist merger. The choice there is obviously to define a new role or continue the gradual drift into oblivion.

Glenwood Presbyterian Church also has reached the end of one era—an era when the dominant role of this congregation was to offer a remarkable ministry to the school-age children of the members. Now most of the members are too old to have school-age children. What is the new role of this church? Who are the clientele for this new role?

If one accepts Glasser's basic point that role now takes precedence over goals, how do the leaders of these congregations, most of whom were reared in a survival or goal oriented culture, go about the process of defining a new role for their congregation? How do they reach and minister to young adults, youth, and children who have been born into a role-oriented culture?

All five of these congregations have been accustomed to planning and decision-making in an era when the congruence of role and goal was not a serious issue. In a survival-oriented culture, goals directed toward survival and growth did not produce role conflicts.

Now in an era when the congruence of goal and role is not automatic, how do congregations such as these plan for the future?

This question is further complicated by the tendency for policies which produce short-term improvements to lead in the long run to disaster.[3] To be more specific, the tendency of congregations, such as First Church and Glenwood Presbyterian, to place a very high priority on a ministry to school-age children and youth tends to produce a high level of satisfactions on a short-term basis and disaster on a long-term basis. Likewise the pattern of moving to a landlord role tends to produce short-term satisfactions and disaster on a long-term basis. In Forrester's terms, the intuitive response to a complex issue tends in the long run to be counterproductive.

Some observers will contend that organization development is the appropriate response to this dilemma. Unfortunately, life is not that simple. The congregation faced with defining a new role for itself must deal with at least four factors. The first almost invariably is the issue of self-esteem. This subject is discussed in greater length in the next chapter.

Second, the leaders must recognize that both they and the congregation as a whole almost certainly have been trained to accept role as a "given" and to

[3] For a lucid and concise introduction to this concept which was first articulated by Jay W. Forrester see Dennis Gabor, *The Mature Society* (New York: Praeger Publishers, 1972), pp. 153-158 and 195-202.

move from that "given" to formulating goals. Today that means putting second things first. This book is an attempt to help leaders identify their congregations in terms of type, past role, current role, and alternative roles for the future. At this point one form of intervention in the organization development process called organizational devolution may be helpful. Regardless of the methodology used, the critical issue is to deal with current organizational behavior patterns.

The next step often is to develop a preliminary or tentative definition of a new role, in other words, begin to articulate a new identity for this congregation. Here the basic methodology of organization development can be very helpful. As this is happening, specific short-term operational goals *which are consistent with this new role* should be formulated. These must be short-term goals. These should be goals which are amenable to an easy and highly visible self-evaluation process. These *must be outreach* goals. The primary focus must be on people who are not members of this congregation or on priorities which are not of a survival or a congregational maintenance nature. As these short-term goals are formulated, achieved, and evaluated, they provide a basis for reflection on the preliminary definition of a new role. They also enhance the capability of the congregation to articulate and accept a new role.

A caution flag should be raised here to warn that the redefinition of role is not an easy task for any organization or institution! The ecclesiastical cemeteries are filled with the remains of congregations, theological seminaries, church related academies and colleges, denominational agencies, councils of churches, ministerial associations, and ecumenical ventures which decided it was easier to die than to define and adapt to a new role.

In more specific congregational terms the difficulties involved in defining a new role can be illustrated by looking at a few of the questions facing St. Paul's

175

Lutheran Church as it moved from an era of youth and growth to a new role as a mature and complex parish.

1. What are the implications for St. Paul's moving from a survival and growth goal orientation to a role orientation?

2. How does this influence the expectations placed on lay officials of the parish?

3. What does this say to the pastors?

4. How will the satisfactions and psychic rewards which accompany the achievement of specific tangible goals which are a part of the youth-, growth-, and goal-oriented era be replaced with equally satisfying and rewarding feelings when the emphasis is on the far less tangible and visible question of identification and fulfillment of role?

5. What does this shift from a goal-oriented era to the role-oriented era say to the retraining of leaders, both lay and clergy, who have had five to twenty years of on-the-job training in a goal-oriented parish?

6. What are the differences in the requirements for leadership needs and skills?

7. What organizational changes are required in the parish which moves from a goal-oriented era to a role-oriented era?

8. As the "contemporary goals" of the 1950s and 1960s become part of the "heritage," how does the mature parish assimilate new members?[4]

9. As a very large parish, such as St. Paul's, moves from the era of youth and growth to the era of maturity and institutional stability, how will the members respond to the idea that this is not "one great big family," but more realistically should be described as "a congregation of congregations"?

10. If one accepts the validity of the first of the three earlier sentences quoted from Glasser's book, what does this say to the mix of longtime members

---

[4] One answer is, "Not very easily!" What are alternative responses to this question? For a conceptual frame of reference for looking at this issue, see chapter one, "Commitment and Assimilation."

and newcomers in leadership positions if this parish is to move from an era distinguished by an emphasis on being a young, growing, and goal-oriented parish into a new era distinguished by an emphasis on role and a distinctive identity?

11. Perhaps most fundamental of all, what is the new role of St. Paul's as a mature and increasingly complex parish in an increasingly heterogeneous community? What distinctive role in ministry is the Lord calling St. Paul's Church to, now that it has reached this point of maturity, strength, and potential?

12. Finally, since institutions tend to change more slowly than do the attitudes and values of people, how does a goal-oriented parish, which for years has projected a pattern of accepting people on the basis of the tasks they perform and on how well they perform these tasks, change its way of relating to people? How does such a parish respond to the nineteen-year-old who simply wants to be accepted, but is not interested in doing anything?

The same basic issue is before Faith Church which once had a distinctive role as "First EUB Church." How does it develop a new identity?

Or, at Glenwood Presbyterian, how does this church relate to mature adults who no longer have children, when for years the relationship between the church and these parents was on their "performance" as volunteer staff in the Youth Club? How does this congregation change its identity from that of a "great youth club church" to one which can offer a challenging and convincing model of adult discipleship?

While these are not easy questions for a congregation to respond to, it is an extremely encouraging sign when they are being asked and given serious consideration. This suggests that the agenda has been changed from survival goals to identity, and at that point it may be appropriate to look at the level of self-esteem.

10
A Beginning Point

Broadway Church was founded in 1889 in what turned out to be one of the most prestigious neighborhoods in the city. By 1927 it had grown to become the second largest church of its denomination in the entire metropolitan area. Old First Church was both larger and stronger, and the two were more or less friendly rivals for the position of *the* leadership church in the denomination in that part of the state. By the late 1940s the continued growth at Broadway coupled with a slight decline at First Church had moved Broadway into the position of being the leading congregation in the denomination in the regional judicatory. Dr. Williams, the senior minister, was a well-known national leader. He had come to Broadway in 1947 after an illustrious twenty-year career in one of the great pulpits of the denomination. When he retired, twelve years later, it was clear that Broadway had begun to slip. The Sunday morning worship attendance, which had peaked at an average of 940 in 1953, had declined to approximately 600. The Sunday school had dropped even more sharply, from an average attendance of 1,120 in 1952 to 480 in 1959. Fifteen years and five pastors later Broadway was a much smaller congregation and morale had dropped even more sharply. As recently as 1957 the staff had included three ordained ministers, a full-time director of Christian education, and a full-time minister of music. By 1965 this had been reduced to two ministers, a part-time Director of Christian Education, a part-time organist, and a part-time choir director.

In 1974 the staff consisted of one minister, one

secretary, a seminary intern, one custodian, and a part-time combination organist-choir director. The average attendance at Sunday morning worship was down to 205. The Sunday school had shrunk to three adult classes, one poorly attended high school class, and one class which included grades two through eight with an enrollment of 26 and an average attendance of 13. Only occasionally did anyone under the age of eight appear for the Sunday school. The entire Sunday school had an attendance of 70 to 80 on a typical Sunday. The receipts for the year totaled $68,000 including $3,900 in memorials and $3,200 income from the endowment fund of $80,000. The youngest active leader was born in 1937, the second youngest in 1931, and the third youngest in 1926. Every other person in a leadership position had been born before 1920.

Individual interviews with persons of influence and in leadership positions elicited these comments. The most pessimistic ones have been eliminated from this list. "Today Broadway is an inner city church, and we might as well face what that means. It means either we begin to get help from the denomination or we close our doors."

"If we had relocated to the suburbs back in 1957, as some of us wanted, we wouldn't be in this mess today."

"Do you see any hope for a small, weak, struggling congregation such as Broadway is today? I sure don't."

"Where we made our mistake was in not getting a first-class pulpit figure when Dr. Williams retired. It's been downhill ever since he left."

"My guess is that Broadway will be closed within five years."

"We're simply too small and too weak to carry on anything except a survival operation here and pray for a miracle. If God has a place for Broadway in his plans, he'll cause that miracle to happen."

"I'm seventy-one years old and not in very good health. My parents were charter members of Broadway, and I've been here since my mother brought me when I was six weeks old. My hope is that Broadway will be able to hang on until after I pass away so I can be buried from here."

"It's too late! If we were going to plan for the future, we should have begun twenty years ago when we could have planned from a position of strength. There's no point in trying to plan from a position of weakness."

"We have a bright and energetic young minister, but what can he do alone? What can you do when your assets consist of a building, a good pastor, a tiny endowment fund, but you don't have any members?"

What is the beginning point in planning for this type of congregation?

———•———

The Maple Grove Church passed its one-hundredth birthday a few years ago. The available records provide statistical data only for the past forty-nine years. During these five decades this open country rural church has fluctuated in size between a peak of 107 members in 1949 and a low of 81 in 1937. Today the membership roll carries the names of 97 confirmed members of whom 17 live outside the county. Worship attendance averages 48, down slightly from the peak of 53 in 1951. The Sunday school attendance has fluctuated between 40 and 60 for over twenty years. Last year the dollar receipts totaled $11,600. This was considerably above both the previous year and the expectations for this year because it included the cost of a new roof on the white frame church building and a $700 repair bill for the heating system. Maple Grove last had the service of a full-time minister in 1951. For the next twenty-one years it was served by a succession of eight seminary students.

This arrangement was terminated in 1972 when the

ancient parsonage was seriously damaged when the furnace exploded. The parsonage was torn down and a month later Maple Grove was yoked with a larger church twelve miles away. These two congregations share a full-time minister who graduated from seminary in 1968. He and his family live in the town in which the other church is located.

The members view this as a very small congregation of very loyal members. It is perceived as too small and too weak to have much program beyond Sunday morning, the women's organization, a vacation Bible school every summer, and special midweek services during Lent.

What is the beginning point in planning for the future of this type of congregation?

————•————

"It was a mistake ever to have started this congregation!"

"This church was established in 1962 in the expectation that a population explosion was going to occur out here. Well, that explosion has never happened, and I doubt it if it ever will!"

"For ten years we had a full-time minister and we didn't grow. I don't see any reason to expect this congregation to start to grow now that we have a half-time pastor."

"We're too small to carry on a full program and our mortgage is too big for the denominational bigwigs to allow us to close. I guess we'll be a tiny, struggling little church forever."

"There ought to be someone in the denomination with the authority to come along and knock little churches like this one in the head and put them out of their misery. We're no good for ourselves and no good to anyone else."

"I was a charter member here and for several years I had real hopes for Southlawn, but I guess we should face reality and either merge or dissolve."

These are representative of the comments offered by leaders at the Southlawn Church when they were asked to appraise their situation. This 120-member suburban congregation was launched in 1962 and quickly grew to a membership of 85. It peaked eight years later at 135 and appears now to have leveled off at approximately 120. During the past few years the worship attendance has fluctuated between 70 and 80. Last year the contributions from the membership totaled $17,000. With the help of a $5,000 grant from the denomination they were able to meet their $980 monthly mortgage payments on the small brick building which was completed in 1965. The financial squeeze, which was intensified by a reduction in the annual denominational subsidy, caused Southlawn to shift in 1972 from a full-time pastor to sharing a minister with another older city congregation of about the same size which has its meeting place eight miles north of Southlawn. For the past four years Southlawn has averaged nine transfers out and six transfers into the membership. One-half of the present membership joined before July, 1966, and one-half have come in since that date.

What is the beginning point for planning for the future in this type of congregation?

These three congregations represent three substantially different types of churches. One appears to be what once was a very prestigious congregation and now is a declining inner-city church. The second is representative of the thousands of small, stable, and thrifty rural churches scattered all across the American countryside. The third is an "arrested development" new suburban congregation, not unlike the teenage church described in chapter five.

Despite the differences in type, these three congregations share one very common characteristic—a very low level of self-esteem. This is a characteristic common to the vast majority of all congregations in American Protestantism. In perhaps one-half of all congregations it is sufficiently serious that it must be given first priority in any serious effort to plan for ministry for today and tomorrow.

The basic reason why this is such a serious problem can be illustrated by this incident and diagram.

You have just had a five-minute conversation with an individual you have never met before. After he has moved away, you are asked to guess his probable life expectancy. Recalling the white hair, the limp, the lined face, and the quivering voice, you first begin to estimate this man's present age and health. You guess he is in his middle sixties and in poor health and estimate he will be lucky to be alive ten years from today.

REALITY

PERCEIVED REALITY

Now you are told this man actually is thirty-nine years old, the white hair is a unique hereditary characteristic, the limp is from a football injury he incurred while playing with his two teenage sons last week, and the weak voice is the result of excessive enthusiasm at last night's high school football game which his sons' team won in the last ten seconds of play after being behind at one point 37 to 9. Now what is your estimate of this man's life expectancy?

Your first guess was based on your perception of reality. Your second guess was based on a substantially different understanding of reality. In both cases you did what any normal person does in looking into the future. You made a projection about the future based on your understanding of reality.

The same process takes place whenever a congregation begins to plan how it is going to respond in faithfulness and obedience to the call to ministry. Projections about possibilities, potentialities, opportunities, and resources are based on the perception of contemporary reality.

In at least one-half of the churches in American Protestantism the *perception* of contemporary reality is so much lower than actual reality that efforts should be taken to narrow this gap before any serious planning is initiated. If this is not done, the plans will be based on an inadequate understanding of the opportunities and resources.

How can this gap be closed?

One easy-to-use beginning point for the next meeting of your church council or long range planning committee is to draw a vertical line on a large sheet of newsprint or on the blackboard and divide it into four sections. The finished product will resemble this.

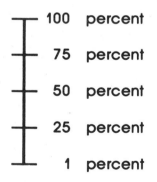

100 percent

75 percent

50 percent

25 percent

1 percent

Explain to everyone this question. "Using average attendance at worship on Sunday morning as the yardstick for measuring size, how does this congregation compare in American Protestantism? This chart symbolizes the range in size of all the congregations in American Protestantism. For example, a congregation that would have more people at worship on Sunday morning than three-quarters of all churches would be located at the 75 percentile line on this chart. Another that would be in the smallest one percentile in size would be located at the bottom of this chart. If one-half of all churches have more people at Sunday morning worship than does our congregation and half have less, then we would say ours ranks at the 50 percentile. Now let's go around the group, and each of you call out the number that you believe describes where our congregation is located on this vertical bar. For example, if you believe 36 percent of all churches in American Protestantism have fewer people at worship on Sunday morning than we do, and 64 percent have more, then call out 36 when it is your turn. If you believe we have more people at worship than do 85 percent of all churches, call out 85."

As the people call out their estimate of size, make a mark on the chart locating where their estimate falls on this scale.

When this was done at Broadway Church, the guesses ranged from a low of 20 percent to a high of 85 percent. All but five, however, were clustered in the 40 to 60 percentile range.

At Maple Grove the range was between 2 and 40 percent, but most of the guesses clustered between 10 and 15 on the scale.

At Southlawn the estimates in response to this question ranged between 5 percent and 40 percent, but most of them clustered in the 20 to 40 bracket.

Now look at the table below and see if this illustrates the point about low self-esteem?

(Note: There are approximately 500,000 religious congregations in the United States. This table is derived from data for slightly over 80,000 Protestant congregations. Because of the nature of the sources it probably is skewed slightly to overstate the number of larger congregations and to underrepresent the number of congregations in the smallest quartile.)

Average Attendance at Sunday Morning Worship in American Protestant Churches

Percentile	Average Attendance at Worship
95%	350
90%	260
85%	200
80%	150
75%	140
70%	130
60%	100
50%	75
40%	55
35%	45
30%	40
25%	35
20%	30
15%	25
10%	20
5%	15

A second method of responding to this issue of self-esteem also can be used at a meeting of the governing body of your congregation. Ask everyone present this question. Let us take about five minutes to reflect silently on the past. While we do this, will you each make a list of five or six significant accomplishments in ministry that occurred in or through this congregation during the past twelve months? Reflect back on what we have been able to do as a congregation in ministry, outreach, and service and simply list five or six achievements of the past twelve months beyond our Sunday morning schedule.

When this was done at Broadway Church, only seven of the nineteen persons present could list as many as five items and three leaders turned in completely blank sheets of paper. A composite list drawn from the sheets turned in produced nineteen different items!

At Maple Grove eight of the twelve leaders had at

least three items, but only the pastor had more than five. The composite list made up *only* from items on these twelve lists produced thirteen different items —and four more were added by telephone the next day. At Southlawn the longest list had five items, three listed four items and there were only two blank sheets turned in. The composite included twenty-six items.

If your congregation resembles the typical church, the respondents will include a few people who are unable to list more than one or two accomplishments in ministry during the past twelve months, perhaps one or two leaders who complete the exercise with a blank list, and several who have only three or four items on their list when time runs out. In the typical congregation, however, an hour's careful review by two or three informed people will produce a list that will have fifteen to fifty significant items on it!

This exercise illustrates one of the most important basic principles in church planning. *The skill which the churches have developed to the highest level of competence is the capability of keeping secrets!*

Lifting the level of self-esteem of a congregation requires breaking this conspiracy of secrecy. This conspiracy of silence will not be broken and the problem of congregational self-esteem will not be solved until the leaders in the churches begin to take seriously the injunction of Jesus recorded in Matthew 5:14-16.

What Will You Celebrate?

The most effective and naturally the most difficult approach to this question of self-esteem can be summarized in the question, "What will you celebrate at the end of this year?"

What are you, as a congregation, planning to celebrate at the end of the year? What blessings granted you as a called-out community of believers during this year will you single out as you give thanks to God? What happened in your church during these twelve months that you want to lift up in celebration? What are your plans for such a celebration next year?

The contributions of time, energy, and dedication by many people to the life and work of your church? The renewed interest by your congregation in sharing in the work of the universal church? The renewal of the spiritual life of your congregation? The completion of a building program? The resurgence of interest by young married couples in your church? The vitality of one of the church school classes? The fact that you will end the year in the black financially? The way the people rallied around one of your members in a time of crisis or sorrow? The new outreach in ministry by your congregation to people in your community who are not members of your church? The birth of seven new babies to members of your congregation? The transformation in the life of one individual who is now an inspiration to many? The retirement from active service after thirty or forty years of hard work by a teacher, a farmer, a nurse, a post-office employee, a doctor, a mechanic, a merchant, a secretary, or a carpenter? The fact that your congregation is still alive? The fact that an alcoholic has been "on the wagon" for six months now? The years of dedicated Christian service by a member who died a few months ago? A new opportunity to share in ministry and fellowship with another church from this community? The response of your congregation to a special offering to assist the victims of a recent disaster? The retirement of the mortgage on the church? The partial completion of a new venture in ministry? A new spirit of unity and brotherhood among the members? The recovery of one member from a very serious operation? The chance for several of the members to share personally in ministry with people from another state or another nation? An increase in the number of young married couples in the congregation? A new

A BEGINNING POINT

format for worship that is especially meaningful for several people? A greater acceptance—or at least toleration—by the members of diversity in values, goals, program, and life styles? A new era that is beginning to emerge in the life of your church school? The arrival of a new minister and family?

You may choose to have this special celebration or worship event at the end of the calendar year. Or at the beginning of the new year. Or in conjunction with the annual celebration of the anniversary of the founding of the congregation. Or at the end of the school year. Or at the end of one part of the program cycle and the beginning of a new program cycle.

In every congregation there are at least two or three attractive possibilities every year for a special event in which the members look back over what has happened and give thanks to God for his gifts and his grace.

There are many reasons for doing this and several are deeply rooted in the history of the Christian Church. The Easter and Christmas services are the two most highly visible examples of special celebrations of thanksgiving by Christians. In the United States the annual special Thanksgiving service is one example. The dedication or consecration of a new building occasionally is another example of a special thanksgiving service.

Today some congregations are holding special celebration events built around four themes. The first is to give thanks to God for the *specific* blessings he has bestowed upon that called-out community of believers. The second is to lift up to greater visibility to all the members what has happened in the life of that congregation during the past several months or the past year. They find this to be necessary since in most congregations today an increasingly large number of members are largely or completely unaware of much that is happening in their midst. The third theme is to recognize and to thank the members and the groups who have carried out special responsibilities on behalf of the total congregation.

Finally, this type of special service lifts up to a higher point the level of understanding of the members of the total performance of that congregation. This is a very important, but often neglected consideration in church planning and goal setting. As was pointed out earlier in this chapter, the expectations of either an individual or a group about the future tend to be influenced very heavily by the perception or understanding of past events or current performance. In nearly every congregation today most of the people, including most of the leaders, have an incomplete knowledge of all that is happening in the life of that fellowship. This means any projections of expectations into the future will be unduly low since they normally are based on an overly modest or inadequate perception of all that is happening in that parish. In simple terms this means that expectations about what tomorrow can bring are raised by increasing the people's understanding of all that is happening today.

These special celebrations take many different forms. In one congregation there is a special two-hour service on Thanksgiving morning that combines a detailed review of what has happened during the past twelve months with a service of praise and thanksgiving.

In another the high school youth group made an 8 mm. motion picture film of what they saw happening in the life of that parish during the year and the "world premier" was shown at this special celebration.

In one parish a series of color slides, skits, tapes, movies, banners, one-act plays, displays, posters, and songs are woven into a special worship service twice a year.

Another congregation has placed the *complete* responsibility for planning and conducting this special service of thanksgiving in the hands of the Men's Club and this is their special project for the year. An incidental fringe benefit is that what was a dying Men's Club now has purpose, meaning, vitality, and enthusiasm. The combination of this new enthusiasm and the nature of this project also have made the Men's Club an effective organization for the assimilation of new members.

In another a group of elderly women gathered one day each week to make quilts, and they spend an hour each day on a special quilt. This special quilt takes a year to complete since one significant event of the previous week is recaptured by the piece of material sewn into the quilt that week. The displaying of this quilt is a part of this annual celebration. In another congregation this annual special service to give thanks for the gifts from God during the past year is combined with an hour devoted to a presentation of the goals and objectives of that church for the coming year.

If you do have such a special service for giving thanks at the end of this year and plan to do this again next year, it will be helpful if you give twelve months notice to those who will be responsible for planning next year's celebration of thanksgiving.

There are two additional fringe benefits that often accompany a direct attack on the problem of a low level of congregational self-esteem. The question, "What happened in this congregation last year?" also serves as a simple test of the quality of the internal communications within the congregation. How well informed are the leaders about what your church is doing in ministry, service, and outreach? This question will provide one indicator. If it turns out that the leaders are not well informed about what is happening, what is the level of awareness of the other members? If most of the leaders are able to identify five or six significant accomplishments in ministry during the past year, it may be helpful to ask this same question of a cross section of the membership. If most of

HEY, THAT'S OUR CHURCH!

the leaders are not able to list more than two or three, the next step may be an examination of the reporting system to determine how it might be improved so more people would be better informed about what is h